Doves in Cr

Iraqi Christian Martyrs

Robert Ewan

GRACEWING

First published in England in 2017
by
Gracewing
2 Southern Avenue
Leominster
Herefordshire HR6 0QF
United Kingdom
www.gracewing.co.uk

ISBN 978 085244 912 7

Typeset by Gracewing

Cover design by Daniel Merrett

In memory of my father, William Avia Ewan,
My first editor

My Lord Jesus, adorn me with the crown of martyrdom,
You know how much my heart longs for it.
You know how much my soul loves You.
Grant me to look with joy at the sword of my executioner.

Mar Shamoun Barsabbae (d. 341)

Contents

Acknowledgments

First of all, I am grateful to Almighty God for giving me the strength to complete the book. I would like to pay special thanks and appreciation to Jeremy Low. His proof reading and editing skills made this book happen. His comments encouraged me to move forward with the book.

I also thank my sister Linda Ewan for her translation and for her commitment to the project.

Foreword

The story of Christian life and worship in Iraq is full of pathos—suffering and pain. As I have seen with my own eyes on numerous visits to the country, pain and persecution have brought the Church to the point of extinction but have also acted as its life-blood, incarnating in the faithful a profound sense of the sacrificial nature of true Christian discipleship.

Robert Ewan has vividly captured the struggle for survival that has characterised Iraq's ancient Christian community down the ages, comparing and contrasting episodes from the earliest centuries of the Church with the chilling instances of persecution that we see today at the hands of Daesh (ISIS) and the like. What emerges are heroes of faith, men and women, young and old willing and able to pay the ultimate price for the truth that they profess in word and deed.

Not so long ago, conventional wisdom routinely banished religion as irrelevant to a post-modern world where self-realisation, science and reason had no place for traditional faith practice. How times have changed. A concurrent theme in Robert Ewan's text is how religious faith continues to have the power to shape and guide an individual's response to life, determining for them what is important, and giving them a sense that truth and love matter more than fame and fortune. In so far as this is true, this book acts as a tribute to timeless virtues of faith, hope and charity that are so firmly imprinted on the history of Iraq but which run the risk of being stamped out by forces that have contorted faith into a mantra of hatred, violence and hyper-extremism.

I warmly recommend this book to all those who want to delve behind the news headlines and catch a glimpse of the soul of Iraq's faithful people.

John Pontifex
Head of Press & Information
Aid to the Church in Need (UK)

Introduction

esus told his disciples: "If the world hates you, remember that it hated me before you" (John 15:18). The world hated Jesus, and they crucified him. In the same way, the world has hated Christ's true followers. Many Iraqi Christians have been killed in the name of Christ through the ages. It is important for us to remember the faithful who deeply loved and followed Jesus into the most dangerous circumstances, with the direst consequences.

Jesus Christ was willing to die and suffer for us, and down through the centuries there have been thousands of believers who have immolated themselves for Jesus Christ. The martyrs resembled the wheat grain that dies on the earth but gives lives to many seeds. "Unless a wheat grain falls on the ground and dies, it remains only a single grain. But if it dies, it yields a rich harvest" (John 12:24–25). They followed their teacher's call before He ascended to heaven: "You will be my witnesses not only in Jerusalem but throughout Judea and Samaria, and indeed to the ends of the earth" (Acts 1:8). They concluded their testimony by giving their sacred blood in an unfathomable surge of courage. Theirs was an allegory of the soul's yearning to be united with Jesus.

The vicious persecution of Christians did not fulfil its purpose—to wipe out Christianity in Iraq—but on the contrary, Christianity flourished. The sight of Christians greeting their martyrdom with elation, preferring the bitterness of death to life without Jesus, arose feelings in onlookers, who were, indeed, often puzzled, and wondered what was the source of the martyrs' courage. The ferocity of the Christians' desire to cling on to their faith shocked those watching. Many of their grudging admirers and unbelievers converted to Christianity.

The dreadful persecutions of Iraqi Christians shows us the awful picture of the depravity of human nature and the unrelenting and insatiable thirst for Christian blood, which still continues to our present day. Men have devised the most brutal, sadistic, and extraordinary forms of torture, and used them against the Christians. This is the ultimate embodiment of evil in men.

How did the Iraqi Christians survive under such severe torments? The incredible fact is that the Christians not only survived, but grew and prospered. They emerged stronger from every suffering. The accounts of these Christian martyrs show the extraordinary resilience that humanity can show in the face of the most extreme circumstances. By learning from their example we can find ourselves strengthened in the trials that we face. Iraqi martyrs have a prominent role in the prayers and shrines of Iraq. Iraqi Christians sing songs of praise at Mass and vespers praising the martyrs' courage. Their shrines and relics are visited by thousands of people to receive their blessing. They represent a living spiritual heritage and paragons of virtue.

What about the Iraqi Christians of today? Since the US-led invasion of Iraq in 2003, thousands have been killed, and over one million have fled Iraq to safer places. Almost 40,000 refugees are in Turkey, 5,000 in Jordan and 10,000 in Lebanon. In the north of Iraq and Baghdad there are 100,000 Christians who were expelled from Mosul and the Nineveh Plains in northern Iraq by ISIS in 2014. Iraqi Christians have been persecuted and uprooted from their own homelands, where they had lived for nearly 2,000 years; they are now facing a systematic elimination of their identity, religion, and culture.

Iraqi Christians have no tribal structure, depriving them of the blood ties that bind other Iraqis together in times of trouble. As such, they have never formed self-defence militias, despite the fact that post-war Iraq offers little reward to those who turn the other cheek.

This book gives brief historical accounts of the many faithful who gave their lives for Christ. It shows the tragedy and brutality of persecution, as well as the unerring confidence of men and women of God who kept the ember of their belief in their hearts. Many martyrs found the wherewithal to overcome cruelty with courage, and they met hatred with an indomitable spirit. They were tortured, their bones were broken, their limbs torn away, and they were beheaded, yet they never succumbed to their tormentors.

This book honours the martyrs whose corpses fertilise the soil of Iraq.

Christianity in Mesopotamia

esus Christ told his disciples: "Go out to the whole world; proclaim the Good News to all creation." And so the Lord Jesus, after he had spoken to them, was taken up into heaven; there at the right hand of God He took his place, while they, going out, preached everywhere (Mk 16:16). After Jesus instructed his disciples and filled them with all the gifts of the Holy Spirit during Pentecost, they went on to preach the good news of the Kingdom of God to all nations.

Christianity entered into Mesopotamia, present day Iraq, during the first century. But as there is no hard evidence that suggests a specific date, we always refer back to the Christian tradition and some of the writings of Church historians. Throughout the centuries, many historians and scholars have offered different theories regarding the introduction of Christianity to Mesopotamia.

The evangelist Matthew mentions at the very beginning of his Gospel an event which marked the marvellous moment of the birth of Christ, namely the coming of the Magi—the Wise Men of the East. The Gospel-writer narrates: "Now, when Jesus was born in Bethlehem of Judea in the days of Herod the king, behold, there came wise men from the east to Jerusalem, saying: 'Where is He that is born King of the Jews? For we have seen His star in the east, and are come to worship Him'" (Mt 2:1–2). The evangelist continues that, after reaching Judea and encountering Herod the tetrarch, these wise men finally arrived at the Christ-child. The evangelist says: "After they had heard the king they departed; and lo, the star that they had seen in the east went before them, till it came and rested over where the young child was" (Mt 2:9).

In his book *Deboritha* ("Book of the Bee"), Bishop Suleiman al-Basri, born towards the end of the 12th century, and appointed bishop of Basra, mentions that the Magi who came from the east to visit Jesus in Bethlehem became disciples of Christianity when they returned home. They were given some pieces from Jesus's swaddling clothes.

According to St John Chrysostom (d. 407 AD): "The Incarnate Word on coming into the world gave to Persia, in the persons of the Magi, the first manifestations of His mercy and light... so that the Jews themselves might learn from the mouths of the Persians of the birth of their Messiah." According to tradition, the Persians had learned of the coming of the Messiah from the prophecies of Zoroaster, who was said to have been a disciple of the prophet Jeremiah during the captivity of the northern kingdom of Israel under the Assyrians in 721 BC. Thus, we see that the prophecy concerning the coming of the promised Messiah was known in the land of the Persians as well. In fact, the great patriarch of the Church of the East, Timothy I (780–823 AD), asserted that it was exactly these Magi who preached the coming of the Messiah in the land of the Persians.

The second major New Testament event concerning the apostolic origins of Christianity in Mesopotamia is the fulfilment of the prophetic event of Pentecost, which took place in the Upper Room fifty days after the Resurrection. Being one of the three 'pilgrim feasts', many Jews were to be found in Jerusalem, having come from different parts of the Roman Empire, and also from beyond the limits of the Roman Empire. St Luke, evangelist and historian of the Primitive Church, narrates in the Acts of the Apostles:

"And there were dwelling in Jerusalem Jews, devout men, from every nation under heaven. Now, when this was voiced abroad, the multitudes came together, but they were astounded because every man there heard the men speak in his own language. And they were all amazed, and marvelled, saying one to another: "Behold, are not all these men who speak Galileans? And so how can we hear every one of them speak in our own tongue, from where we were born? Parthians, and Medes, and Elamites, and the dwellers in Mesopotamia and in Judea, and Cappadocia, in Pontus, and Asia..." (Acts 2:5–9).

Thus we can see that there were Persian Jews present in the Holy City for the feast of Pentecost who heard the preaching of the apostles, and especially this is related in the narrative of Peter, and they received the Gospel of Jesus Christ: "...then they that gladly received his word were baptized; and the same day there were added unto them about three thousand souls" (Acts 2:41). It is highly likely that these Persian Jews took back with them to their homeland the Gospel of Jesus Christ, thus sowing the seeds of the Gospel among their fellow Jews in the Diaspora, as well as among the non-Jewish inhabitants within the Persian Empire, which was at that time the second superpower after the Roman. There are, however, a number of secondary sources that chronicle the spread of the Gospel to Mesopotamia. According to the tradition of the Church in Mesopotamia, the disciples who preached in the area were four: St Thomas, Addai, and Addai's disciples Aggai and Mari.

The Doctrine of Addai

An important document narrating the establishment of Christianity in the Aramaic-speaking East was written in

Aramaic, and came down to us in its final form sometime between 390 and 400 AD; its contents are certainly earlier than the date of its writing.

This document chronicles the coming of Addai (Thaddeus), believed to have been one of the Seventy-Two disciples (Lk 10:1) sent by Saint Thomas, one of the Twelve, to the small kingdom of Osrhoene, or Edessa, which is present day Urfa in southeast Turkey. The Doctrine of Addai contains the letter of Abgar inviting Jesus to visit Addai's kingdom, and the Lord's response promising eternal life to the king and the inhabitants of his kingdom for believing in Christ's name.

The Church historian Eusebius, Bishop of Caesarea (c. 264–340 AD), narrates what many scholars have called the 'legendary' letter of Abgar V, King of Edessa, to Christ, seeking healing from his illness. The letter is quoted in Eusebius's Historia Ecclesiastica (I, 13:5–10). Eusebius is said to have visited Edessa sometime in 323 AD, where he is alleged to have found the records of the letters in Syriac, which he most probably used as sources for his history of the events. He states regarding Abgar, who heard of the preaching and divine healings wrought through Christ, that "In this way King Abgar, the celebrated monarch of the nations beyond the Euphrates, perishing from terrible suffering in his body that was beyond human power to heal, when he heard much of the name of Jesus and of the miracles attested to unanimously by all men, became Christ's supplicant and sent to Him word by way of a letter, asking to find relief from his disease."

The *Historia Ecclesiastica* of Eusebius then continues to narrate the outcome of the letter and the mission of Addai, who is identified with Thaddeus, one of the Twelve in the Syriac version (cf. Mt 10:3), and one of the Seventy-Two in the Eusebian tradition.

Even though the letters were condemned as 'apocryphal' in the West by Pope Gelasius in 494 AD, the Syriac-speaking churches of the East certainly considered them to be founded upon historical truth. The famed theologian St Ephrem the Syrian (ca. 306–373 AD) refers to the Abgar tradition, though not necessarily to the letters themselves, in his Testament: "Blessed is the town in which you dwell, Edessa, mother of the wise; by the living mouth of the Son has it been blessed by the hand of His disciple. That blessing will dwell in it until the holy one reveals himself."

The multicultural city of Edessa was thus from early on evangelised by apostles from Jerusalem, and the existence of Jews in the city provided the crucible for the growth of the faith of Christ, and the existence of merchants and silk-traders provided the personnel for apostolic work and the spreading of the faith. It is most probable that Christianity started first in Urha and then spread southward towards Mesopotamia.

Acts of Mari

Further minor documents, such as the Acta Maris, or Acts of Mar Mari, are from a much later period, and describe the missionary activity of Mari, the disciple of Addai, into Seleucia-Ctesiphon, which became the seat of the Church of the East in 280 AD. According to the Acts, Mari is supposed to have founded over 300 churches or communities, and is said to have been buried at Deir Qunni, which was known as one of the foremost pilgrimage sites and 'basilicas' of the patriarchal see. However, even though this tradition cannot be corroborated by any documentary evidence outside of the Church's tradition and later documents, it nonetheless demonstrates the importance of the oral tradition in attempting to explain the origins of what has been called the most missionary-minded Church in all Asia.

In addition to lower Mesopotamia, Mari evangelised in Arbil and where Kirkuk stands today. Arbil is known to have had a bishop at a very early stage of Christianity in Mesopotamia. Mari is also believed to have spent some 35 years in his evangelistic mission in Mesopotamia, including some ten years in al-Ahwaz (the south of Persia). By the time of Mari's death, the Christian religion was spreading throughout the region, with an ever-growing multitude of converts developing into a new community of worshippers. The attitude of the Persian rulers varied between hostility and tolerance.

The Testimony of Bardaisan

Another early witness to the Abgar tradition is the Book of the Laws of Countries, written by the Gnostic Bardaisan (154–222 AD) sometime at the beginning of the third century. Bardaisan was born in 154 AD in Edessa to supposedly pagan parents, and was brought up by a pagan priest. Sometime in 179 AD, at the age of 25, he became a Christian when one day he passed by the church founded by Addai and heard the Scriptures read and interpreted; he was soon baptised by Hystasp, the bishop of Edessa, and ordained deacon by him.

Bardaisan also mentions the presence of Christians in Parthia, Gilan (southwest of the Caspian Sea), Bactria (between the ranges of the Hindu Kush and the Oxus), Persia, Edessa and Media, and by the year 200 AD knew of the presence of Christians over the known parts of Asia.

The Evangelisation of Adiabene

Arbela, which is present-day Erbil in northern Iraq, was the capital of Adiabene, a small Persian border kingdom and the earliest centre of Christianity in Iraq. The first-century Jewish historian Josephus mentions that a king of Adiabene accepted Judaism around 36 AD. Such a conversion made Arbela a natural centre for a Jewish Christian mission at an early date. Christianity spread both in villages and cities, and by the end of the Parthian period (AD 225) Christian communities were settled all the way from Edessa to Afghanistan. The Chronicles of Arbela report that by this time there were already more than twenty bishops in Persia, and that Christians had already penetrated Arabia and Central Asia.

Addai is also believed to have been the apostle of the region of Adiabene. With the presence of a great Jewish diaspora, and the fact that Syriac was also the tongue of Adiabene, the connection with missionaries from Edessa is almost indubitable. Whether by Addai himself or a disciple, the tradition points to Edessa as being its source of evangelisation. Furthermore, the cities of Edessa, Nisibis and Adiabene were connected by the Silk Road, and the Jewish, Christian and pagan constituencies of these cities lived side-by-side; the strong Jewish presence allowed for the swift progress of Christianity throughout these merchant centres.

Tatian the Assyrian (120–175 AD)

Tatian was one of the most famous Christians of Adiabene, who produced one of the earliest verifiable historical pieces of evidence for Christianity in the Far East, in Persia. Tatian was a philosopher and biblicist who refers to himself as being from 'Assyria', hence the Latinized form of his name, Tatian Assyrus. According to S. H. Moffett, this remarkable biblical scholar, linguist and ascetic was born of pagan parents in the ancient Assyrian territory of northern Mesopotamia (modern-day Iraq) that was Adiabene. He converted to Christianity, later becoming a disciple of Justin Martyr. He is the famous compiler of the Diatessaron, or 'harmonised' Gospel—which he probably composed in Syriac, and which was used by all of the Syriac-speaking Churches in the East up to the time of its suppression by Rabbula, the West Syrian bishop of Edessa, sometime after 411 AD.

The testimony of Egeria the Iberian (c. 384 AD)

A very important witness to the tradition of the apostolic activity and missionary work of Saint Thomas is the so-called journal of the late fourth-century Iberian nun Egeria. Egeria's famous journal records her pilgrimage to the Holy City and various other pilgrimage-sites visited by the Spanish nun on her journey. She recalls:

> No Christian who has achieved the journey to the holy places and Jerusalem will also miss going on the pilgrimage to Edessa. It is twenty-five staging posts away from Jerusalem. But Mesopotamia is not so far from Antioch. So, since my route back to Constantinople took me back that way, it was very convenient for me at God's bidding to go from Antioch to Mesopotamia (*Pilgrimage of Egeria*, 17:1).

But God also seemingly moved her with a desire to go to Syrian Mesopotamia [the Greek translation of the Padan Aram of Gen 28:1, which Egeria uses in reference to Edessa]. She writes: "The holy monks there are said to be numerous, and of so indescribably excellent a life that I wanted to pay them a visit; I also wanted to make a pilgrimage to the martyrium of the holy apostle Thomas, where his entire body is buried" (*Pilgrimage of Egeria*, 17:1). The holy bishop told her that "King Abgar wrote a letter to the Lord, and the Lord sent his answer by the messenger Ananias."

The Tent Priests

During the third and fourth centuries, many Christian monks and priests played a major role in spreading Christianity across the Iraqi desert. Some of these priests accompanied the nomad Arabs in their travels throughout Iraq and the Arabian Peninsula. They were called the "The Tent Priests." They converted the tribes of Taghlib, Abbad and Bakir, which used to travel south of Kufa in Iraqi and north of the Arabian Desert. Some of these priests built monasteries along the trade routes that acted as resting places for the merchant caravans.

Koukhi—first church in Iraq

oukhi was the first church built in Mesopotamia (Iraq). It was constructed during the latter half of the first century and became the seat of the Patriarchy of the Church of the East, which it remained up until the tenth century.

One historical account relates that Mari (who was converted to Christianity by Addai, one of the seventy disciples of Jesus) arrived at Ctesiphon, a city built during the Parthian dynasty (247 BC-224 AD), at some point between 79 and 116 AD. After settling in Ctesiphon or nearby Seleucia, Mari (later Saint Mari) continued to preach the gospel, and performed several miracles by curing the sick. Mari was able to take possession of a temple outside the city of Seleucia which had been used by Zoroastrians—worshippers of fire. He converted this temple into a church. The pagans, fearing for their religion, complained against Mari to Artaban, the Parthian king.

The king then brought Mari before him, threatening dire consequences if Mari continued to worship the Christian God instead of the god of fire. Then, King Artaban revised his approach, and tried to test this new faith by asking Mari to cure his sister who was ill. This Mari duly did by a miracle, and immediately seized this new opportunity and asked the king's sister a favour: to grant him ownership of the temple of fire on the Tigris River. The king's sister quickly and readily told Mari he could keep the temple of fire as his church. This pagan temple became the Church of Koukhi. It is believed that this first church was established possibly around 80 AD at the heart of the

Parthian dynasty power base. After this, by the end of the first Christian century, according to ecclesiastical tradition, St Mari had founded over 300 convents and churches in Seleucia-Ctesiphon.

The name Koukhi derives from the Aramaic word "Koukhi", meaning hut or cottage, because there were many Christian farmers in this area who lived in huts. The building that St Mari established was not a large structure, but was a chapel-size house attended by parishioners for praying and celebrating feast days. He built two more churches, one at Dorta and the other at Dari Kani, where he was buried.

The church of Koukhi soon became the official seat of the Catholicos and, later, the Patriarch of the Eastern Church, and played a major role in the development of the Eastern Church. The influence of the bishops of Koukhi began to increase, and the Patriarch of Koukhi regarded himself as the highest Church authority.

By the time of Shapour II, who came to the throne in 309 AD, Christianity had become the favoured religion of the Roman emperors. Constantine the Great even claimed a protectorate over all Christians everywhere, and in 315 AD wrote to Shapour II requesting that Shapour give special protection and favours to Christians. This sparked the beginning of 40 years of persecution of Christians by the Sassanids. The Sassanids destroyed all Christian places of worship, and Koukhi was not spared; the Christians were forced to worship in secrecy until the violence subsided and they were able to rebuild their Church.

In 363 AD, Jovian, the Roman Emperor, concluded a treaty with Shapour II. By this treaty, Mesopotamia and Armenia came under the control of Persia. Temporary peace was established. In 409 AD, the Persian king Yazdegard, by an edict of toleration, brought an end to the persecution of Christians. This allowed the Christians to re-organise.

Koukhi then once again became the official seat of the Eastern Church, and played a major role in its development; the number of bishops began to increase, and the Patriarch of Koukhi assumed the highest authority and adopted the title "Catholicos" and, later, Patriarch.

The church of Koukhi was rebuilt again between 415–420 AD, financed by generous grants from the Roman Emperor Theodosius II. It was further extended by Patriarch Mar Abbae I between 550–551 AD, and more renovations continued in the ensuing years. Patriarch Mar Abbae issued a decree that all future Patriarchs must be ordained in Koukhi. The church was now in constant use, and several synods of the Eastern Church were held in Koukhi. Up to 25 patriarchs were also buried there, the first being Apres (121–123 AD) and the last being Hananeshoo II in 779 AD.

In the middle of the eight century, the Abbasids took control of the Arab empire. In July 766 AD, after four years of rule, Caliph Abu Ja'far Al-Mansour completed the building of the city of Baghdad. He believed that Baghdad was the perfect capital of the Islamic empire. Mansour loved the site so much he is quoted as saying, "This is indeed the city that I am to found, where I am to live, and where my descendants will reign forever."

It is likely that it was the largest city in the world at the time, with several estimates suggesting that the city contained over a million inhabitants at its peak. The patriarchs at Koukhi realised that they were now far away from the centre of power and influence, and made a strategic decision to move the seat of the Eastern Church to Baghdad. The seat was relocated from Koukhi to Baghdad by one of the greatest patriarchs of the Eastern Church, Timothy I. He believed that understanding the Abbassid rule and mentality was vital for the Church and its growth. He believed that the Church had to play an important part in the growth of society in Baghdad, contributing to it its knowledge of medicine, philosophy and translation.

Despite moving the patriarchal seat to Baghdad, Koukhi remained at the heart of the Eastern Church. It was a traditional habit of the newly ordained Patriarch to visit the shrine of Mar Mari, and to be ordained in Koukhi and then return to Baghdad.

During the Mongol invasions, destruction reached Koukhi and the surrounding areas. The patriarchal seat was transferred to Irbil (northern Iraq), after which it was relocated continuously. Koukhi was destroyed, and as time went by its significance became a forgotten past. Most of the buildings collapsed bit by bit and were covered in dust and sand.

National and the foreign archaeological missions have often tried to discover the ancient monuments of Mesopotamia. During attempts to discover the city of Seleucia-Ctesiphon, both a German expedition (1927–1932) and an Italian expedition (1964) carried out archaeological digs in the area. Together, they have helped discover the location of Koukhi.

The church is located on the right side of the road passing the Doura slaughterhouse (south- east of Baghdad), through the farms and then out to the area of the Jubori Arabs. About 25 kilometres from the slaughterhouse there is a crossroads leading to a hill. This hill, which is about 12 metres high, is known as the hill of "The daughter of the judge." If a person stands on top of the hill he will be able to see the remains of the church.

The present state of the ruins of the church is pitiful. The road to the ruins is a dirt road difficult for cars. People have to walk for 1.5 kilometres to the location of the church. The remains are covered with weds and scrub.

The Persecution of Iraqi Christians

he Parthian Empire (247 BC–224 AD), also known as the Arsacid Empire, ruled over Mesopotamia (present-day Iraq) for two hundred and fifty years. The Parthians were too religiously tolerant to persecute the Christians, and their less tolerant Sassanian (226–641 AD) imperial successors, were too busy fighting Rome. Moreover, as long as the Roman emperors considered Christians to be enemies of Rome, the Persian emperors were inclined to regard them as friends of Persia.

At the time of the persecution of Christians in Rome, many Christians sought refuge in Mesopotamia, and were often given protection by successive Parthian and Sassanian rulers. Christianity steadily grew in Mesopotamia, partly due to the deportation of several hundred thousand Christian inhabitants of Roman Syria, Cilicia and Cappadocia by Shapour I (240–270 AD). The deportees settled in Mesopotamia and Parthia. This settlement was based on economic and demographic reasons, but it also unintentionally promoted the spread of the new faith. The Zoroastrian priesthood was still hostile towards its religious rivals, including Christians. They viewed Christianity as the work of the devil, just as the Christians in turn viewed their rival religions. Persecution of Christians within the Sassanid Empire was ongoing, with Christians reported as welcoming martyrdom.

Many Christians were employed in large-scale construction projects, and there were considerable numbers of skilled workers and craftsmen among them. Some cities soon became significant cultural and educational centres, such as Jundaishapour, famous for its library and university and home to scholars from all over the Persian Empire, many of whom were Christian and Jewish. Jundaishapour also became the centre of silk weaving in Persia, with many Christians involved in every aspect of production, management and marketing. This period of peace and prosperity for the Christian community lasted until the reign of Bahram II (276–293 AD), when Christianity again suffered. Its chief opponents were the Zoroastrian Magi and priestly schools, as well as some Jews. The Zoroastrian church, meanwhile, suffered the loss of thousands of its believers, from all ranks of society, who converted to Christianity.

On 28 October 312 AD, Emperor Constantine met Emperor Maxentius in a battle just outside the city of Rome at the Milvian Bridge. This battle was one of the most important events in the history of Christendom, since it was through Constantine's victory that Christendom began to be truly established.

Eusebius of Caesarea, a Christian biblical scholar and historian who wrote the first biography of Constantine soon after the emperor's death, knew Constantine well, and said he had the story from the emperor himself. Eusebius wrote: "Before the Milvian Bridge battle, Constantine and his army saw a cross of light in the sky above the sun with words in Greek that are generally translated into Latin as 'In hoc signo vinces' ('In [the name of] this sign conquer'). That night, Constantine had a dream in which Christ told him he should use the sign of the cross against his enemies. He was so impressed that he had the Christian symbol marked on his soldiers' shields."

The next day, 28 October 312 AD, Constantine defeated Maxentius's army. Maxentius himself drowned in the Tiber trying to escape. Such was the beginning of Constantine's embrace of Christianity, and such was the beginning of the conversion of the Roman Empire from paganism to Christianity.

The conversion of Constantine to Christianity, and the adoption of the faith as the state religion of the Roman Empire early in the fourth century, placed Christians in Mesopotamia under immediate suspicion as potential traitors, and paved the way for future persecutions, which continued in Mesopotamia, where they had started in the first place, for a century after they had ceased in Rome. According to Eusebius, Constantine himself wrote to Shahpur II, warning him that in 260 AD Shahpur had been allowed by God to defeat Valerian because the latter had persecuted the Christians. This ill-advised letter was written about 315 AD, which probably triggered the beginnings of an ominous change in the Persian attitude toward Christians. Constantine believed he was writing to help his fellow believers in Persia, but actually succeeded only in exposing them to increased persecution.

Faced with what seemed to be a double threat, a threat not only to national security but to the national religion as well, Persia's priests and rulers cemented the alliance of state and religion in a series of periods of terror that have been called the worst persecution of Christians in history, "unequalled for its duration, its ferocity and the number of martyrs."

For the next two decades and more, Christians were tracked down and hunted from one end of the empire to the other. At times the pattern was one of general massacre. More often, as Shapour decreed, it was an intensive, organized elimination of the leadership of the Church—

that is, the clergy. A third category of suppression was the search for that part of the Christian community that was most vulnerable to persecution: Persians who had been converted from the national religion, Zoroastrianism.

Shapour was not the only enemy of the Christians; in the Chronicles of Arbela, Christians blame Magi, Jews, and Manicheans for promoting hatred against Christians, calling them Roman spies. Some Christian accounts of the martyrs show the Jews in a bad light, and this is also true of some writings of the Eastern Church fathers.

In 340 or 341 AD, the new Metropolitan (Archbishop) of Ctesiphon, Shamoun (Simeon) Barsabbae, was urged by Shapour II to collect a special tax from the Christians to finance the costs of the war against Rome. His refusal was the prelude to the systematic persecution of Christians. In the Martyrology of Simeon, Shapour is quoted accusing the bishop of political motives.

Inciting the anti-Roman political motivation of the government's role in the persecutions was a deep undercurrent of Zoroastrian fanaticism and hatred of other religions. The zealots' hatred, and the type of charges they customarily hurled against Christians, can be seen in the following passage from one of the Acts of the Martyrs, which quotes a royal decree:

"The Christians destroy our holy teachings, and teach men to serve one God, and not to honour the sun or fire. They teach them, too, to defile water by their absolutions; to refrain from marriage and the procreation of children; and to refuse to go out to war alongside the Shah-in-Shah. They have no scruples about the slaughter and eating of animals; they bury the corpses of men in the earth; and attribute the origin of snakes and creeping things to a good God. They despise many servants of the King, and teach witchcraft."

Sometime before the death of Shapour II in 379 AD, the intensity of the persecution slackened. Tradition calls this the forty-year persecution, lasting from 339 to 379 AD, and ending only with Shapour's death, but the worst seems to have been over at least a decade before his death. Perhaps it was the great Persian victory and the crushing defeat and death of the invading Roman emperor Julian in 363 AD that brought a period of peace to the Church in Persia.

On the death of Shapour II in 379 AD he was succeeded by his brother and then his son, Shapour III, in 383 AD. Shapour III did not wish to continue with the policy of persecuting the Christians. He freed Christian prisoners, believing they would be of greater value to him pursuing their crafts and paying taxes. Shapour III died in 388 AD and was succeeded by his son, Bahram IV. In 399 AD, Bahram was succeeded by his brother, Yazdegerd I.

In 409 AD, the Persian king Yazdegard I, by an edict of toleration, brought an end, for the time being, to the persecution of Christians. He had a Jewish wife, and was well-disposed towards both Judaism and Christianity. The Zoroastrian priests were displeased. They spoke of 'Yazdegerd the Wicked'. And he was called the 'Christian King' by some. The edict allowed Christians to worship in public and to build churches. The peace helped the Christian community to re-organize its life. Tensions eased further when Persian Christians created their own ecclesiastical organizations with their own hierarchy, and the Persian Church eventually became independent from the Western Church.

But the persecutions, it would seem, had never really ended. Like smouldering coals, hatred and fanaticism were always just beneath the surface of the volatile social order, as Wigram describes it: flaring up from time to time, then "flickering out" again, but persisting up into the first years of the fifth century. It is said that in Bishop Qayuma's time the persecutions were still so intense that when he was asked as an old man of eighty to accept the perilous position of leader of the Church, he accepted only because, as he said, "I am going to die soon anyway, and I had rather die a martyr than of old age."

When at last the years of suffering ended, around the year 401 AD, the historian Sozomen, who lived near enough to that time of tribulation to remember the tales of those who had experienced it, wrote that the multitude of martyrs had been beyond enumeration. One estimate is that as many as 190,000 Christians died during the persecutions. It was worse than anything suffered in the West under Rome, yet the number of apostasies seems to have been fewer in Persia than in the West, which is a remarkable tribute to the steady courage of Asia's early Christians.

The Zoroastrians had more luck with Yazdegerd's son, Bahram V, who became known for his prowess in hunting game—and women. Bahram V attempted to win and maintain goodwill for himself with the Zoroastrians, and in 421 AD the persecution of Christians resumed. Many Christians fled westward to the Roman Empire, and Bahram sought their extradition. But the Roman emperor at Constantinople, Theodosius II, himself a Christian, refused Bahram's request.

Bahram V responded with another war against the Roman Empire. Constantinople overpowered Persia's forces in a series of skirmishes and Bahram made a hundred year peace in which he agreed to grant freedom of worship for Christians in the Sassanid Empire, in exchange for Constantinople granting freedom of worship for Zoroastrians under its rule.

When the Islamic call started in Arabia, Patriarch Isho'yahb I (595–581 AD) sent gifts to the Arabic prophet in the form of 1000 silver drapes. According to the 'Book of al-Sa'aradi', they were taken by Bishop Gabriel of Prath d'Maishan, but by the time he arrived at his destination the prophet was already dead. They were given to Caliph Abu Baker al-Siddiq. It is said that there were agreements and pledges made at that time between the Muslims and Christians, but historians doubt this, as there is lack of good evidence.

During the first half of the 7th century, Muslim rule in southern Mesopotamia was firmly established. When the Muslims arrived in the area, around 632 AD, they were welcomed by the Christians of Iraq. Many people from the Arabian Peninsula were of Christian descent, and they took part in battles and worked in the administration of the Caliphate. As a reward for their services, it is reputed that Christian Arabs were exempt from the Zakat tax.

The battle of Qadiysia (636 AD) was the decisive turning point between Arab and Persian rule in Iraq. In the aftermath of this battle, many skirmishes occurred; and eventually Seleucia-Ctesiphon (present-day Mada'an) was conquered by Saad ibn Abi Waqas. The Christians of Iraq faced several challenges caused by the resurgence of Islam and the migration of Muslims to Mesopotamia (due to the large influx of people from the Peninsula, some monasteries were occupied and used as living quarters). As a result of continuous battles in the area, a state of anarchy prevailed within the Archbishoprics of Mesopotamia and the Gulf.

Some Christians converted to Islam, as they saw similarities between the two faiths, such as Judgment Day, the Resurrection, reverence for the Virgin Mary, prayers, fasting, and alimony. There was a resemblance between the language of the Muslims (Arabic) and the Christians (Aramaic), as both were of Semitic origin. Moreover, old links existed to a number of Christian Arab tribes who lived in the Arabian Peninsula long before the advent of Islam. The majority of the Iraqi Christians adapted themselves positively to the new situation. Muslim leaders relied on them to administer the affairs of their rule (as most Muslims were engaged in fighting). Many Christians lived in relative peace during the four Muslim Caliphate rules. They were allowed to participate in commerce and social life. General Saad even asked them to join him in planning the city of Kufa, and they were allowed to live there in peace. He did not allow any destruction of churches, and these were permitted to ring their bells any time, day or night, except during the call to Muslim prayers. This peaceful policy of co-existence allowed the Christians to learn the Arabic language and its grammar, and then they started to translate science and literature into the Arabic language. Later caliphs, such as Omar ibn al-Khatab and Ali ibn Abi Talib, continued in this tolerant policy towards the Christians.

When Muawiya ibn Abi Sufyan established the Umayyad Caliphate (661–750 AD) he also followed tolerance towards the Christians, and gave some politically sensitive positions to Christians, such as Mar Yohanna al-Damashqi, who controlled the finances of the empire, and his personal doctor, Ibin Aathal, was given the responsibility for collecting taxes. His personal curator was a Christian by the name of Sargon. On one occasion, a Christian was made the governor of the prison of Kufa. During this time, Christians obtained some high positions within the Islamic empire.

The Abbasid Caliphate (751–1258 AD) overthrew the Umayyads and moved the Caliph's seat from Damascus to Baghdad. The Abbasid caliphs followed the same pattern of their Umayyad predecessors; Christians continued to hold important positions at the Caliph's court. The rise of the Abbasid Caliphate led to the Islamic Golden age, sometimes known as the Islamic Renaissance, lasting until the 13th century. During this period, the Muslim world became an unrivalled intellectual centre for science, philosophy, medicine, and education, as the Abbasids championed the pursuit of knowledge.

The head of the Church of the East became the official representative of the Christians to the Abbasid Caliphate. In the ninth and tenth centuries, members of the Church of the East played a significant role at the court of the caliph, gaining respect in particular as personal physicians and court doctors, and amassed great wealth. One such was Gabrail, who was the personal physician of the fifth Abbasid Caliph, Harun al-Rashid (786–808); Gabrail became very wealthy. The monasteries educated an outstanding new generation of civil servants. Some monasteries were visited regularly by government officials during Christian festivals. The Caliph Harun al-Rashid visited the monastery of Mar Zakka, and Caliph al-Ma'mun stayed at the monastery of Michael, near Mosul.

The period between the rule of Abū al-'Abbās as-Saffāḥ and Al-Mu'tasim is often regarded as the golden period of Iraqi Christians. There was a high level of tolerance for Christianity, and many churches and monasteries were built. Thousands of Christians had jobs in government. Muslims celebrated Christian feast days; for example, the Feast of the Cross became a public holiday, and Palm Sunday was celebrated by Muslims alongside Christians. Many Christians were rich as result of their professions, such as in pharmaceuticals and medicine, and they worked in free trade and agriculture. Some of them owned grand and lavish houses. The Caliphs grew accustomed to inviting Christian theologians to discuss their faith with the Muslim men of sacred learning, the Mutakallimun (doctors of the science of the word), and some of these discussions were later published.

As a result of the victories of the Byzantine emperor Leo IV, Caliph al-Mahdi (775–85 AD) had many churches destroyed. The Christians were accused by the Caliph of praying day and night for the triumph of the Byzantines. As a result, many Christians migrated to the Byzantine Empire and settled there, and those who remained behind were viewed with suspicion by the Muslims.

In the time of Caliph Al-Mutawakkil (847–861 AD), many churches were destroyed. Al-Mutawakkil was unlike his brother and father in that he was not known for having a thirst for knowledge, nor for showing religious tolerance. He issued strict directives to the Christians, such as:

1 Ringing of church bells was prohibited.

2 Reciting of the psalms in public was forbidden.

3 Displaying crosses in public was forbidden.

4 Building over any formerly Muslim property was forbidden.

5 Public funerals were banned (usually the deceased's family would say loud prayers and sing mourning dirges on their way to the cemetery).

6 Riding on horseback was forbidden.

7 Use of saddles was banned when mounting an ass or a donkey.

As a result of these oppressive laws, some Christians converted to Islam and others migrated to the north of the country. There were daily harassments, which incited people to attack Christians. On the other hand, some Christians paid little attention to this maltreatment and continued to translate texts and teach in medicine, astrology, and pharmaceutics, and especially philosophy, which had a great amount of influence on the development Islamic thought.

There are even examples of a few Christians who were employed in responsible and sensitive positions. The Caliph al-Mu'tasim (833–842 AD) employed two Christians who were his personal confidants. No legal documents were valid until signed by Sulmuyah and his brother Ibrahim, who were also set to administer the public treasury. The Caliph was overwhelmed with grief on the death of the latter.

Al-Mu'tadid (892–802 AD) had as the governor of Anbar the Christian Umar b Yusuf. Al-Muwaffaq, who was virtually the ruler during the reign of his brother Al-Mu'tamid (870–892 AD), entrusted the administration of the army to a Christian named Israel. His son al-Mu'tadid (892–902 AD) had as one of his secretaries another Christian, Malik b al-Walid.

Although by the mid-1200s much of the glamour and importance of Baghdad was fading away, the caliphs were figureheads more interested in worldly pleasures than serving God by serving the people. The Abbasid army was effectively non-existent, and only functioned as bodyguards of the Caliph.

After the Crusades that came from the West, which shook the stability of the Islamic world during the 11th century, a new threat came from the East during the 12th century: the Mongol invasion. In 1257, the Mongol ruler Mongke Khan resolved to conquer the Abbasid Caliphate. He conscripted one out every ten fighting men in the empire into his invasion force. This force, by one estimate 150,000 men strong, was probably the largest ever army fielded by the Mongols. In November of 1257, under the command of Hulagu and the Jalayir general Koke Ilge, and the Chinese vice-commander Guo Kan, set out for Baghdad. The army lay siege to the city, starting on January 29. On February 10, Baghdad surrendered. The Mongols swept into the city on February 13. A full week of pillage and destruction commenced. The Mongols were indiscriminate, destroying mosques, hospitals, libraries, and palaces. It is estimated that between 200,000 and 1,000,000 people were butchered in that one week of destruction. The Mongol Hulagu's Christian wife, Dokuz Khatun, successfully interceded with her husband to spare the lives of Baghdad's Christian inhabitants. The Christians saw the Mongols as avengers of oppressed Christianity; they were pleased with the fall of the capital of Islam.

When Patriarch Dinkha I, head of the Eastern Church, died in 1281, the bishops elected a Mongol successor by the name of Yahballaha III. This was a political election, as it was extremely rare for an outsider to become Patriarch; however, he was elected because of his supposed influence with the Mongols. He received a seal that his predecessor had been given by the great Khan Mongke. Bishops, priests, and other notables were not to approach the great Khan without a letter bearing this seal. It can be seen on a 1302 letter to Pope Boniface VII, as well as one to Benedict XI dated 1304. For some forty years the Iraqi Christians lived under Mongol rule.

The Jalayirids were a Mongol Jalayir dynasty which ruled over Iraq and western Persia after the breakup of the Mongol Khanate in the 1330s. The Jalayirid Sultanate lasted about fifty years; all the remaining churches, schools, and Jewish synagogues were either converted into mosques or destroyed. Christians were forced to pay the Jezia tax. However, sources do not mention any physical damage being inflicted on them.

In 1370, the empire of Timur Lenk (Tamerlane) rose in Central Asia, with Samarkand as its centre. During his campaigns, thousands of Christians were slaughtered, bringing about the de facto destruction of the Church of the East in Central Asia. Tamerlane's campaign of conquest had the character of a "Holy war". Baghdad fell to him on 9 July, 1401. Anarchy, plunder and slaughter descended upon the cities and villages of Mesopotamia. Many surviving Christians escaped towards the northern cities of Iraq. Hundreds of churches and monasteries were deserted and became a nesting place for crows and owls. Subsequently, even the Christians of northern Iraq were not spared the carnage.

A curtain of darkness engulfed the north, just as it did the middle and south of Mesopotamia. In light of the unimaginable atrocities, it is difficult to believe that there are a handful of monasteries and churches in Iraq which survived Tamerlane's era. The Church of the East never recovered from this disastrous period. No major scholarly and spiritual institutions remained.

The Ottoman Turks under Sultan Suleiman entered Baghdad in 1534, and from then on Baghdad and Iraq became a dominion of the Ottoman Empire. The Turks utilized the millet system, which permitted individual religious and ethnic groups broad rights of self-governance under the guidance of an ecclesiastical leader who was required to collect taxes and enforce the laws. Under this system, the Patriarch of the Church was the highest authority amongst the Christians. Ottoman religious tolerance was notable, and they did not condemn other religious groups.

The Ottoman Empire constantly formulated policies to balance its religious problems. The Turks adopted a policy of giving Muslims more rights than Christians and Jews in order to encourage conversion. For example, only Muslim subjects were allowed to testify against Muslims in court. Of course, there were incidents of outright persecution, such as the destruction of many villages in the Nineveh plain by Tahmasp (1514–1576) of the Safavid dynasty. In 1832, atrocities were committed against the Christians by Muhammed Merkoor, prince of Rawandouz (northern Iraq).

Many Assyrian Christians in northern Iraq were subjected to Kurdish brigandage and even outright massacre and forced conversion to Islam, such as the massacres inflicted by Badr Khan in 1846. He attacked the Christians, destroyed their villages and killed many of them and many more were captured and sold as slaves throughout the Middle East. These massacres drew international attention through the western press; the revelations also woke European politicians and public opinion to the plight of Ottoman Christians. This led European countries to pressure the Pope to intervene and stop the massacres. An Ottoman army was sent to the region in 1847; it clashed with the Kurds in several battles that ended with the arrest of both Badr Khan and Nurallah, and led to their exile in 1850.

The Assyrian genocide known as Sayfo or Seyfo (' The Sword') refers to the mass slaughter of the Assyrian population of the Ottoman Empire and those in neighbouring Persia by Ottoman troops during the First World War, in conjunction with the Armenian and Greek genocides. The Assyrian civilian population of upper Mesopotamia was forcibly relocated and massacred by the Ottoman army, together with other armed and allied Muslim peoples, including Kurds, between 1914 and 1920, with further attacks on unarmed fleeing civilians conducted by local Arab militias. Since the Assyrian genocide took place within the context of the much more widespread Armenian genocide, scholars and historians rarely treated it as a separate event. Estimates of the death toll vary from between 100,000 and 300,000 people. Some of those murdered were Iraqi Christians comprising Chaldeans, Assyrians, and Syriacs and other religious dominations. The Christians of northern Iraq, southeast Turkey, northeast Syria, and northwest Iran suffered a genocide which accounted for the deaths of up to 65% of the entire Christian population.

The Ottoman Empire, which included the provinces of Baghdad, Basra, and Mosul, entered World War One on the side of the Central Powers (Germany and Austria-Hungary), and immediately became a target for British imperial ambitions; by March 1917 the British army had captured Baghdad. Iraq remained a satellite of Britain for the next three decades under the terms of the Anglo-Iraqi Treaty, which was signed in June 1930.

Britain decided to try and maintain control in its mandated Iraqi territories through air power. As a result, the RAF recruited a force from the local population, primarily Christian Assyrians, to relieve the British and Indian troops. The force was called the RAF levies. The Assyrians were renowned for their great discipline and fighting qualities. They displayed, under conditions of greatest hardship, steadfast loyalty to their British officers.

The Royal Air Force Station Habbaniya, 55 miles west of Baghdad in Iraq, was the British Empire's most important military base in Iraq. It was also known as the 'Second London'. The vast base included the Air Headquarters of RAF Iraq Command, a RAF hospital, a RAF Levies barracks, and the RAF Armoured Car Company depot, as well as fuel and bomb stores. The station was a large flying training school during World War Two, as well as a transport staging airfield.

The Assyrians did not share an amicable relation with their neighbours. Their historical feud with the Kurds was centuries old. Bitterness between the Assyrians and the Arabs had been reported by British historians as far back as 1920. This was made worse by the British officers of the Levies, who encouraged the Assyrians to think that they were first-class troops; this had the effect of increasing the natural pride of the Assyrians. This, coupled with the fact that the British and Assyrian Levies succeeded in suppressing Kurdish revolts wherever the Iraqi Army had failed, created an inferiority complex among some Iraqi corps in relation to the British and the Assyrians.

The conclusion of the British mandate of Iraq caused considerable unease among the Christian Assyrians, who felt betrayed by the British. For them, any treaty with the Iraqis had to take into consideration Assyrian desire for an autonomous position similar to the Ottoman millet system. The Iraqis, on the other hand, felt that the Assyrian demands were, alongside the Kurdish disturbances in the north, part of a conspiracy by the British to divide Iraq by agitating its minorities. In the year of Iraq´s formal independence, 1933, the Iraqi military carried out a large-scale massacre of the Assyrians (the Semele massacre), who had previously supported the British colonial administration.

After the Second World War, Baghdad witnessed a mass migration: the Iraqi Christians. New Christian neighbourhoods sprang up like al-Doura, which attracted middle-class families. Al-Doura became one of the biggest Christian communities in Iraq, home to more than 5000 Christian households. At its zenith it was home to some 150,000 Christians.

Late evening on the 13 July, 1958, the 20th Brigade of the Royal Iraq Army headed south, supposedly towards the Iraqi-Jordanian border. At 2:30 am it stopped six miles from Baghdad, but instead of swinging south towards the border it headed for the heart of the capital. A few hours later, Iraqis woke up to hear the radio announcing the overthrow of the monarchy and the birth of the Iraqi Republic. Far from ending the revolutionary process, the coup marked a beginning of deeper crisis. Factional splits between the Kurds in northern Iraq and the central government surfaced. In 1960, agitations slowly grow amongst the bellicose Kurds, leading to a full-scale revolt and open warfare. Several Christian villages and dioceses were burned and pillaged.

The Christians continued to progress and grow under the shadow of Saddam Hussein's almost secular state. The adherents of all faiths were kept in check and were able to coexist in relative peace, creating a tranquil interfaith relationship. It is a sad fact that even under his philosophy of terror and his despicable rule, Christians felt safe.

Despite the fact that Saddam was a totalitarian ruler, he banned most anti-Christian activities. But in the north of Iraq, as a result of the Kurdish revolt against the central government in Baghdad, the Iraqi Army destroyed dozens of Christian villages between 1968 and 1990, especially near the border with Turkey.

In 1980 the Iran-Iraq War started, which lasted for eight years, making it the 20th century's longest conventional war. Coffins of Christian soldiers killed in battle arrived almost daily. Grieving parents and relatives would gather around to mourn their loved ones.

In 1986, after six years of war with Iran, and as a result of the influence of Islamic Sunnis in Saudi Arabia and the Shi'ite regime in Iran, Saddam began using Islamic symbols, and affirming that he lived an Islamic lifestyle (or fundamentalist Muslim) to ensure his regime's survival. The consequences affected Christians badly. Iraqi Christians had no clans and were unarmed, so their communities were very weak between 1991 and 2002; they were thus targeted by some Muslims, who kidnapped girls or wealthy businessmen and highly educated Christians.

On 2 August, 1990, Saddam Hussein invaded Kuwait. Units of the elite Republican Guard, spearheaded by the Hammurabi Division, reached Kuwait City within five hours. This action triggered the first Gulf War. After the failure of diplomacy, the allied ground attack began on February 24, 1991, and four days later a ceasefire took effect. As a result of allied bombing during the war, a near-apocalyptic level of destruction fell upon the civilian infrastructure and its institutions. Additionally, the United Nations imposed economic and financial sanctions on Iraq, lasting thirteen years. Those sanctions were regarded as the toughest and most comprehensive sanctions in history. With the Iraqi economy in tatters, leading to high unemployment and inflation and a general hopelessness, the tide of life ebbed away from the Iraqi people; many thousands of Christians left Iraq for better living conditions abroad. It is estimated that almost 250,000 Christians left Iraq.

In April 2003 the allied invasion of Iraq commenced, and Saddam Hussein was ousted. After the invasion, waves of unprecedented cross-sectarian terror burst, with the main groups of Sunni and Shia determined to exterminate each other. These groups viewed the American-led invasion as a Christian crusade, and Iraqi Christians as its supporters and collaborators. As Iraq continued to lose all semblance of order, the persecution of Christians increased in its ferocity, taking the form of bombings, kidnappings, and the killing of women and men; the clergy, the elderly and children were not spared.

After IS (Daesh) stormed Mosul in 2014, they tagged all the Christian homes with the letter N for 'Nassarah', the term by which the Koran refers to Christians. One Friday, a warning was read out in Mosul's mosques and broadcast throughout the city on loudspeakers. It offered Christians three choices: convert to Islam; pay the Jizya, a form of tax; or leave their homes. If they refused these options, they faced nothing but the sword. Many fled the city and chose the uncertainty and hand-to-mouth existence of the displaced. For the first time in the history of Iraq, Mosul is now empty of Christians; over 160,000 Christians were made homeless.

It is estimated that since the Iran-Iraq War some one million Christians have either migrated or been displaced from their lands. It is a crime against an indigenous people with a culture spanning thousands of years. It is a crime against humanity. The Chaldean Catholic Patriarch Louis Sako's words about the plight of the Iraqi Christians still echo in the air: "We feel forgotten and isolated. We sometimes wonder, if they kill us all, what would be the reaction of Christians in the West? Would they do something then?"

1

Sultana Mahdookhet

In the 9th year of the reign of King Shapour of Persia (318 AD), Christianity was widespread across the Persian Empire, with many zealous leaders, one of whom was Mar Abda, the archbishop of the town of Karbat Galal. Mar Abda tirelessly encouraged the persecuted Christians to stay faithful and devout in their faith in the face of hardship.

At that time, in the land of Dersas lived Prince Folar, follower of King Shabour. In accordance with the king's orders, Prince Folar tortured and killed Christians in his district. Prince Folar had a beautiful daughter called Sultana Mahdookhet, and two handsome sons called Edwarferwa and Mehernarsa. He took great care to give them the best scientific and religious education of their day and was immensely proud of them.

On their way back from an introduction to the king's Prime Minister (Ameen), they were galloping on their horses when the youngest son, Mehernarsa, lost his balance, fell from his horse and broke his leg badly. Sultana Mahdookhet and Edwarferwa were terrified and distressed by his fall and took their brother to Ahwan, a small village nearby. A great commotion accompanied the arrival of the brothers and sister, which was noticed by Mar Abda, who happened to be visiting the village at the same time. He set out to visit the injured Mehernarsa, even though he was a pagan.

Meanwhile, Mehernarsa had fainted and a great vision appeared to him. He saw Jesus Christ sitting on a majestic throne surrounded by angels and saints and two solemn men holding Christ's hands, one on each side. Mehernarsa turned to the men and asked them in fear, "who is this man and the men paying homage to him?" The men answered him: "this is the mighty Jesus Christ, eternal king, surrounded by angels and his devout followers and saints." The two men then led Mehernarsa into a sinister darkness and showed him deep wells of fire and sinners suffering, then led him back to Jesus just at the moment when the devout bishop, Mar Abda, was walking towards Jesus. He kneeled down at Jesus' feet and prayed to Him to spare the life of Mehernarsa. The two angels helped Mar Abda to his feet and told him his wish had been granted.

When Mar Abda reached the place where Mehernarsa had fainted and was seeing this vision, he prayed to God among the villagers and straightened the injured leg, made the sign of the cross over it and shouted loudly for Mehernarsa to awake in the name of Jesus Christ, the son of the living God. Mehernarsa rose immediately and walked, feeling fully recovered. All the villagers started shouting in joy and amazement at this miracle.

Mehernarsa recognised Mar Abda from his vision and implored him to baptise him and teach him the Christian faith. His siblings, amazed at this miracle, were also filled with the Christian spirit and asked Mar Abda to lead their dead souls to the light. Mar Abda was overjoyed by their faith and baptised them and gave them Holy Communion.

After the celebrations ended, the spirit of God lifted the siblings from the village and placed them in a narrow cave not far from the village. This miraculous arrangement delighted the siblings, and they decided to live and die in the cave as God willed.

News of what had happened in the village and the disappearance of the siblings reached their father, who in turn notified King Shapour of Persia. Prince Folar sent search parties to look for his children for several months, but they never found them.

As for the brothers and their sister, they were content to live in the humble cave for the next three years, constantly praying and giving thanks to God for their simple life. God gifted them with the ability to see into the present and the future.

When the time finally came for them to be martyred, they became aware of it, and Edwarferwa saw in a vision that Mar Abda knew the location of their cave and was on his way to visit them to give them the last rites before they died.

When Mar Abda reached the cave, he gave them Holy Communion, and encouraged them to be brave in their last days on Earth and to pray for their elderly father. But Mehernarsa said to the bishop, "Dear father, you pray for us, as you will reach Jesus three days before us." Sultana Mahdookhet said, "yes, pray for us saintly father, because our persecutors will reach us in seven days, and on the 15th day we will be martyred." Mar Abda was astonished by their insight, and hugged and kissed them as he bid them goodbye.

The 7th day after Mar Abda's visit, Prince Folar's horse escaped from his stables and reached the cave; the siblings recognised their father's horse and wondered who would follow it. Soon afterwards they saw two stable boys from their father's palace following the horse. The siblings went inside the cave and kneeled in constant prayer. When the stable boys reached the cave and saw three people praying, they were mesmerised by the sight and remained motionless for an hour, unable to speak or move. After they finished praying, the siblings spoke to the stable boys and asked them why they were standing there in wonder.

When the stable boys recognised the prince's children, they bowed to them. Edwarferwa told the stable boys to leave and tell the prince that they had found those he had been searching for without success—lost until God wished them to be found. The stable boys rushed out, but one of them hid in the vicinity of the cave to keep an eye on the siblings in case they moved from their location, while the other hurried back to the prince.

After sunset, a heavenly light glowed in the darkness as two angels descended into the cave to tell the praying saints to be brave in the face of their looming ordeal. When the hidden stable boy saw the light, he approached the cave to sneak inside, but a spark of fire struck him; this was so that he would know that what happened was real, not a vision of his imagination. The boy ran frightened, with his skin charred from the fire.

By that time, the other stable boy had reached the prince and told him about the missing children. Thirty knights were sent by the prince to return his children, and word was sent to King Shabour that the children had been found. The king sent word to the prince to ask for his daughter's hand in marriage because he had heard of her beauty.

When the knights approached the cave they were met by the stable boy struck by fire , who warned them about entering the cave and showed them his burnt skin. But they disregarded his warning and proceeded. When they reached their destination they could hear the saints praying, but could not see them. They set up camp until morning in the hope of seeing more clearly in daylight.

The next day the saints could see their father's knights touching the walls of the cave like blind men, looking for the entrance, but not able to find it. The knights were bewildered because they could hear the saints but could not see them. When the knights did not return the next day, Prince Falor took his guards with him and set out for the valley of the cave. On his way there he met with the returning knights, who begged for his forgiveness for failing to return his children. He asked them to ride back with him until they were a small distance from the cave. When the cave was within sight, the prince ordered his men to fetch the children immediately. At that instant the convoy heard the voices of the children praying, and immediately the horses froze in their tracks and could not move further. The prince was amazed by this and ordered his men to dismount and go on foot. Like the horses, the men's feet froze, and they could not step forward. The prince ordered three bowmen to shoot arrows at the cave, but the arrows took the men's palms with them and bounced backwards.

At this commotion, three bright lights appeared from the cave, and the prince recognised his children. He cried out, calling on them to return to him, and pleaded with them to stop humiliating him in the kingdom of Persia. His children answered him that they had found a better father whom they could not deny, and asked the prince to return home and wait six days until King Shabour's prime minister (Ameen) and his guards arrived, and then to come back to them to complete what was destined.

On the 6th day the king's prime minister, Koshtazad, arrived with seven officers and set out with the prince to the cave. There they found a large crowd of the sick gathered around the cave asking for help. Koshtazad parted the crowd and reached the cave and greeted the saints in

the name of the king. He did this twice, but the saints ignored him and continued to pray for the sick. Koshtazad
was angered by their behaviour and threw a stone at them,
but this bounced back and hit his brow and cut him.
Koshtazad bandaged his head and remained silent until
the prayers were finished. When the saints had asked for
all the sick to be healed in the name of God, everyone in
the crowd was healed, including Koshtazad, who had been
suffering from gout and had three paralysed fingers in his
left hand.

Koshtazad started thanking God and was amazed by
what happened. He asked to speak to the saints without
the crowd and in the presence of their father and the king's
officers only. He then asked them to return back with him
to the king and denounce their Christian faith and be rewarded by the king, who wanted to marry the sister, Sultana Mahdookhet. But they refused to obey.

Koshtazad sent a letter to the king to advise him of
what had happened. The king was enraged by their rejec-
tion and accused them of using witchcraft to remain free.
He sent his magicians to defeat them and soldiers to capture and crucify Mar Abda.

The letter arrived on the 12th day of the incident, and
when the king's soldiers arrived to capture Mar Abda in
his village they found him already dead. When they went
to the cave, the saints already knew what had happened
and told the soldiers to bring the king's magicians to do
their witchcraft.

While the magicians spent two days and nights creating
evil concoctions and praying to their evil gods to kill the
saints, people continue to gather around the cave and the
sick kept coming to be healed. One such person was a 40-
year-old man, blind from birth, who asked to be taken to
the saints to be healed; when the soldiers blocked his way,

he picked up a stone and threw it at the soldiers. The instant the stone hit one of the soldiers his vision returned and he could see again.

When the magicians failed to kill the saints, despite their efforts, the saints prayed to the heavens in loud voices and asked God to humiliate the devil and his followers and to glorify His Church and His worshippers; instantly a fire ignited from the earth and consumed the magicians.

On the 15th day of these events the saints were ready to face Jesus, and asked their father to send his soldiers to take their lives. Their father cried bitterly, but did as he was told. He sent his soldiers to behead them one by one. Soon after they died, their bodies disappeared, and the pagans were unable to burn them as they had intended.

A church has been erected in the place of their martyrdom, and each year their anniversary is celebrated in Araden.

2

Brothers Jonah and Brikhisho

In the 18th year of the reign of King Shapour II of Persia (327AD), Shapour made a major policy decision: he ordered the persecution of all the Christians within his domain and their forceful conversion to the Zoroastrian religion. Churches were demolished and monasteries set ablaze, and he imposed higher taxation on Christians. The king believed that this action would force the Christians to renounce their religion and worship Fire, Sun and Water. Anyone refusing to recant their Christian faith was punished and tortured to death.

During these turbulent times, in the village of Bethassa lived two brothers by the names of Jonah and Brikhisho. When they heard the news about where the Christians were being tortured, they immediately left their village and headed to the place where they were being held. Upon their arrival, the brothers visited the jail where a large number of Christians were imprisoned. The brothers encouraged the prisoners to remain loyal to the Christian faith, and gave them courage in their gnawing anxiety.

There was an aura about the brothers that radiated inspiration to their imprisoned colleagues. Many saw this as the reason why the Christians refused to repent and convert despite their gruesome torture. The actions of the brothers enraged the governor, who ordered the brothers to be brought before him; and he said to them: "I ask you under oath and in the name of the King of Kings to speak truthfully: will you worship the Sun, Fire and Water and give alms according to our king's customs?" The brothers replied:

> We ask you, gracious governor, who have been appointed by the king to govern with fairness and honesty, that you should not fear your king, who appointed you as a governor of this region, but fear the King of Kings, God of Earth and Heavens, who lives throughout the ages, who gives wisdom to rulers to set the laws and rule justly. We ask you under oath, who do you think we should worship? The everlasting creator, or the king who will one day die and be buried with the rest of his ancestors?

Their reply enraged the governor and the leader of the priests, especially when they heard that their king was mortal and would die. They brought spiked wooden cages and imprisoned the brothers separately so that they would not hear each other's testimony.

They asked Jonah first, whether he would worship their god or endure the severe and gruesome torture that they would inflict on him. Jonah refused to denounce his Christian faith, and, quoting Jesus, he said: "whoever acknowledges me before men, I will also acknowledge him before my Father in heaven. But whoever disowns me before men, I will disown him before my Father in heaven. So start whatever you want to do, because we will never give up our faith and spoil the Church of Christ." And he added: "You are the salt of the earth. But if salt loses its flavour, how can it be made salty again? If we succumb to your will then we will be guilty of failing our Christian faith and all the followers who died for their faith."

On hearing Jonah's reply, the governor was incandescent with rage. He ordered Jonah to be tied up and whipped relentlessly, but Jonah tolerated the pain and continued to pray, and thanked God for his faith and asked God to give him strength to endure his pains. With a voice brittle with emotion, he cried out loudly, "I denounce the pagan king and his followers who serve Satan. I denounce the sun, fire, water, the moon and stars, and only believe in the Father and the Son and the Holy Spirit." The ferocity of his defiance shocked his torturers, and they continued to beat him harder, and then dragged him out and left him in the shivering snow.

The following day it was Brikhisho's turn to be tortured. They asked him to renounce his religion, as they said his brother had, or face an excruciating torture. With unerring confidence, he replied:

> I strongly and faithfully worship my God, just like my brother, and stop telling me lies about my brother's renouncing his religion. I would never worship that which God has created to serve his people; how do you expect me to worship what was create to serve humanity, and not the one who created the universe and does not need human help? God said, "I give life and I take life; no one can be saved from me. I am the first and the last, I am who I am."

When the high priests heard what Brikhisho had to say they were amazed by his determination and the strength of his faith. They decided not to try him publicly, as they feared he might influence others by his strong faith. Reeling from the humiliation of their failure, they brought two heated copper balls and placed them between Brikhisho's armpits. They also forced him to stand on two heated plates. They told him that if he dropped the balls, he would be blaspheming against his God. Brikhisho replied: "In the name of Jesus Christ the Son of God I will gladly suffer what you are putting me through. Because to suffer bravely I will secure a place in the Kingdom of Heaven. I beg you to torture me harder." His valiant and robust determination to bear the cruellest torments irritated his torturers. They melted some lead and poured the liquid into his eyes and his nostrils. He was dragged to prison and hung upside-down from one leg.

Then they brought Jonah and asked him, sarcastically, if he enjoyed sleeping in the freezing cold. Jonah replied: "Throughout my life I never had a better night than last night, as I experienced the suffering of Christ." They told him that his brother has blasphemed against his God, but he did not believe them, and said: "My brother has denounced evil and his followers."

Immediately they fell upon him, and they cut all his fingers and toes and threw them in the soil and said: "we will plant your fingers and toes and you will harvest many in their place." Jonah replied: "I do not want any hands, because God who created me will give me wings instead." So they brought a large pot of heated tar and skinned Jonah's head and cut his tongue out and threw him in the pot, but nothing happened to Jonah. When they saw this, they placed him in a device which squeezed him hard until his bones were crushed. He was cut to several pieces and dumped in a dry and guarded well.

The guards brought Brikhisho and told him to have pity on his body, which soon would be smashed to pieces. He replied: "I did not make my body, and my creator will avenge me on the ignorant king who does not know his creator and only follows his own wishes." The guards pulled several of his body parts asunder and poured hot tar on them, and then they set them on fire. Both brothers were martyred on the 29 January, 328 AD.

3

Mar Mehna and the six martyred virgins

In the year 328 AD, the Christians of Karkh Slookh (present day Kirkuk, northern Iraq) were greatly persecuted and were subjected to torture; their churches were demolished and their wealth confiscated, and many of them were pursued and killed.

Bishop Mar Mehna of Karekh Slookh and a number of Christians went into hiding in a small place called Khassan. They built a number of small houses; Mar Mehna would perform Mass and give Holy Communion to his followers. However, they were soon discovered and hunted down like wild beasts; they were tortured and asked to convert from Christianity to worship the pagan gods of the sun and give offerings to the elements of water and fire. When they found Mar Mehna unmovable from his strong beliefs and refusing to swap the truth of God for pagan customs, they stoned him to death.

In the same town, there were six virgins who had travelled from the capital city to this small town. They were called Tekla, Danak, Dhadhoon, Mama, Amzakeyah and Anna, and they pledged their life to Christ.

The Manicheans—followers of the Mani religion—reported the virgins to the governor, who ordered them to be brought to his court. When they were in his presence, he ordered them to be married and to worship the sun. However, they refused to worship anyone else but Jesus Christ, the one true God of heaven and earth, and refused to give up their virginity to anyone. They were taken to a place outside town called Whoora and executed according to the governor's instructions.

After their death, a fig tree grew in the place of their martyrdom that bestowed many miracles on its visitors. This enraged the Manichaeans, and they frantically started cutting the tree and burning the surrounding area to stop visitors from visiting the place. But the just God, who does not tolerate insults to his faithful, inflicted a disease on them.

The place became known as Beet Tina (the House of the Fig), and a large crowd of worshippers would gather every year to say Mass and sing hymns to commemorate the death of the virgins, and they thanked God for all the miracles that he bestowed upon them.

4

Mar Shamoun Barsabbae

He was born in Susa on the Iranian Iraqi border. The exact date of his birth is unknown, but it is thought that he lived for over 117 years. His family was in the profession of dyeing the cloths of kings and princes of the Parthian royal family. He was called Barsabbae, meaning 'son of the dyers'. This nickname stuck with him, as he dyed his body with the blood of his martyrdom.

Sometime during the fourth century he became a disciple and later deacon of the Patriarch Fafa (the head of the Church of the East). He was sent by Fafa as Fafa's representative at the Council of Nicaea in 325 AD (a council called by Emperor Constantine I to establish a consensus in the Church through an assembly that represented all Christendom). In 329 AD he was elected Patriarch of the Church of the East.

The increased tension between the Zoroastrian Persian Empire and the Christian Roman Empire had an adverse effect on the Christians of Persia and their king, Shapour II; some of the king's religious advisors especially began to see the Christians of the land as outsiders and spies, since they shared the religion of the king's enemies. They went as far as accusing the Patriarch of the Church, Mar Shamoun, of being a personal spy for Caesar.

In the spring of 341 AD, Shapour II issued a decree ordering all Christians to pay double taxes to fund his wars with the Romans. He knew that the majority of the Christians earned a low income, and were unable to pay these new taxes. Shapour's order, preserved in one of the anonymous accounts of the martyrs, illustrates the absolute, arbitrary power of the Persian emperor. It states:

> When you receive this order of our godhead, which is contained in the enclosure herein dispatched, you will arrest Shamoun, the chief of the Nazarenes. You will not release him until he has signed this document and agreed to collect the payment to us of a double-tax and a double tribute for all the people of the Nazarenes who are found in the country of our godhead and who inhabit our territory. For our godhead has only the weariness of war while they have nothing but repose and pleasure. They live in our territory [but] share the sentiments of Caesar our enemy.

Mar Shamoun refused to be intimidated. He branded the tax unjust and declared:

> I respect the king's order and obey his will as much as I can, but I have no rule over the Christian people in matters of state; my role is to guide them and lead them in their spiritual lives. We all pray for the king to prosper and wish that peace will prevail during his reign. However, I ask you most humbly, why are Christians expected to pay double taxes? We are not rich, and we do not fail to serve the king and pray for his well-being and follow what our books advise us, to be faithful to our rulers and kings.

Shamoun's response infuriated the king. He gave him another chance to concede, and wrote back to his officials in Arameen to warn Shamoun that his boldness would cost him and his people their lives. He threatened to wipe the Christians off the face of the earth if his rule were not obeyed. Shamoun offered himself as sacrifice in place of his people, to die by any means the king chose to kill him, rather than let his people suffer.

The king was further enraged by Shamoun's unfaltering decision; he roared in anger and felt a strong desire for vengeance and destruction. He immediately commanded the rulers of Arameen to seize Shamoun, and ordered the destruction of churches and the execution of clergy who refused to participate in the national worship of the sun. Shamoun remained unperturbed by the news and continuously prayed to God. He was granted three days to travel to the king's town to present himself. Shamoun was gladdened by this decision; he gathered his priests and deacons and preached to them to remain strong and faithful to their religion, as Christ had been in the face of His persecutors, to distance themselves from pagans and to follow the commandments of God, and to endure pain and death in the name of the Holy Cross.

The crowds were reduced to tears by his words; they were deeply saddened knowing they would be losing their wise leader and good shepherd, and worried they were doomed once he left them, never to return. But Shamoun reproached them and silenced their worries; he hugged and kissed his followers and reassured them that they would be protected at all times by their faith in Jesus.

The king questioned Shamoun's loyalty to him and accused Shamoun of ingratitude after he had raised him to a high rank within his kingdom, saying he had always spoken well of him in front of his advisors and religious leaders. The king blamed him for encouraging disobedience and revolt among the Christians, and said he expected them to pay double taxes to help him in his military campaigns. Shamoun kneeled in front of the king and replied: "our bodies, our lands and possessions are all at the king's mercy; he may take as he sees fit, but I cannot order my people to pay more taxes even if the king were to skin me alive." The king said: "forget the taxes for now and listen to my advice, because I do not wish to kill a wise man like you. My good advice to you is to do as I command you and worship the sun and fire." Shamoun said, "this is the worst advice anyone can give me for my life, and I refuse to follow it."

The king continued to warn Shamoun that if he did not respect him in front of his court and worship the sun and moon and fire then he would be condemning thousands of Christians, who would be killed after him, to death. This did not change the venerable bishop's mind, and he remained resolute and unwavering in his replies.

Patriarch Shamoun, along with 103 prisoners, was chained and dragged to prison for one more night, to give him a last chance to change his mind.

In the morning of Good Friday, 341 AD, Shamoun and his followers were called to the king's palace and told once again to worship the sun to spare their lives. At that, the Christians rose up and refused to accept any such deliverance, seeing it as shameful. So, on the 6th hour on Good Friday, and as our Lord was led to His final hours, Shamoun, five bishops and one hundred priests were led outside the city of Susa and beheaded before His eyes, and last of all he himself was put to death at the 9th hour. His feast day is celebrated by some Iraqi churches on the 21 August of each year.

Mar Shamoun's prayers

Two of his prayers—'A Prayer before Martyrdom' and 'The Crown of Martyrdom'—were written shortly before his execution.

A Prayer before Martyrdom

Lord Jesus, You prayed for those who crucified You
You teach us to pray for our foes
You accepted the spirit of Estepanous, who prayed for those
who stoned him
Accept my spirit and the souls of my brethren
Forgive the sin of the persecutors of your people
Lord, grant them the grace of conversion
Lord, bless the towns and cities You entrusted into my care
Protect all our faithful; consider them like the apple of your
eye
May they find shelter under the shadows of Your wings
Till these troubles pass away
As you promised, stay with them till the end

The Crown of Martyrdom

My Lord Jesus, adorn me with the crown of martyrdom
You know how much my heart longs for it
You know how much my soul loves You
Grant me to look with joy at the sword of my executioner
Grant me peace in Your kingdom, and let Your glory be my
strength
Permit me not to live in this world and witness my people's
hardship
Permit me not to live and see
Your churches demolished
Your altars torn down
Your Holy books ripped
Your holiness defiled
Your anguished monks tortured
Permit me not to live
To see the wolves ravaging your glorious eparchies
Permit me not to live
And see my deceiving friends turning upon me as my exe-
cutioners

5

Tarbow and her sister

arbow was sister of the martyred Patriarch Mar Shamoun Barsabbae. She was renowned for her beauty and elegance. When the queen fell sick with a severe illness, some of her ladies-in-waiting falsely advised her that Tarbow and her sister had cast an evil spell on the queen to avenge their martyred brother. The king ordered their capture, along with their young servant, who was being converted to Christianity by the two sisters.

Two of the king's senior men and his chief governor were sent to question them, but as soon as they saw Tarbow they were overcome by her extraordinary charm. The three men secretly desired her and hid their feelings from each other. The women were accused of bewitching the queen, and were told that they deserved to be killed for their crime. Tarbow replied to this accusation by saying:

> On my life, I don't know what we have done to deserve this false accusation. We are devout Christians who worship God and follow His scriptures. Our scriptures tell us to denounce witchcraft and witches, so how can you imagine that we would be involved in sorcery, when our religion condemns it and prohibits its practice? If you are thirsty for our blood, we are at your mercy; kill us now in the name of our God and not because we blasphemed and concocted witchcraft.

The king's men were overwhelmed by her intelligence and eloquent answer and secretly intended to save her from death for their own selfish desires. They now accused Tarbow of plotting to kill the queen in order to avenge the death of her brother, but Tarbow had another clever reply for them, saying:

> We would be crazy to avenge our brother, when
> you have not caused him any harm. By killing him,
> you gave him eternal life in the kingdom of heaven.
> A kingdom that will destroy your transitory world,
> your false pride and fleeting dominance.

They accused sisters were not killed straight away, but instead were sent to prison overnight. The chief governor sent word to Tarbow, telling her that if she married him he would plead her case to the king and obtain pardon for her. Tarbow was agitated by this request and chastised him for his insensitive remarks; she intended to keep herself pure and marry only Jesus. She gave the same reply to the other two noble men when they asked her to marry them.

The rejected men were humiliated by her response and ruled that the women were witches and deserved to die. They informed the king of their judgment, who initially hesitated and gave the three accused the opportunity to worship the sun in order to save their lives. But that infuriated Tarbow and her sister, and they refused to worship anyone but their creator and love anyone else but Jesus Christ. After that response, they were condemned to death as witches and ordered to have their bodies cut to pieces, allowing the queen to walk between their body parts for healing.

The accused women were taken outside the city to the place of their execution; each was tied to two stakes and sawn in two; each half, thus separated, was cut into six parts and thrown into so many baskets, which were hung on two forked stakes and placed in the figure of half crosses, leaving an open path between them. The queen and her guards walked slowly between the dismembered bodies, hoping that the imagined spell would be cured. No sight could be more shocking or barbarous than this spectacle of the martyrs' limbs cruelly mangled and exposed to scorn. This took place on May 5, 341 AD.

6

Shahdost

he name Shahdost is Persian for a devotee and a friend of the king. Indeed, Shahdost was a faithful devotee to the true king, Jesus Christ. He was born in the village of Beth Germai (present day Kirkuk, northern Iraq), and was one of the archdeacons of Patriarch Mar Shamoun Barsabbae. Three months after the patriarch's martyrdom, he was secretly elected as the new patriarch of the Church of the East, based in Seleucia-Ctesiphon (central Iraq).

The synod of bishops convened a clandestine meeting to elect a new patriarch, and after several days of deliberations Shahdost was unanimously elected. He willingly accepted his election, knowing that it might lead to his death. He appointed many priests and bishops to replace the ones who were martyred. They pledged themselves to die on behalf of their flocks, and went out and encouraged the faithful to stand firm and resist the perfidy of Shapour.

Two years later, Shahdost was arrested. Three days before his arrest he had seen in a dream a ladder with its foot on the Earth and its head in heaven. Mar Shamoun was standing at the top of the ladder wrapped in glory and joyfully saying: "Shahdost, climb up to me on this ladder and don't be afraid. I climbed it yesterday and you will climb it today." Shahdost was convinced that the dream meant that he would die soon. When he told his dream to the faithful, they grieved for him.

Three days later he was arrested in Seleucia-Ctesiphon together with 128 priests, deacons, monks and nuns. They were thrown into prison for five months, subjected to tortures and urged to embrace the religion of the Magi, but they remained firm in their faith.

The satrap of Seleucia-Ctesiphon then ordered 120 of them to be killed—all men—but he sent Shahdost along with the nuns to Shapour. When the patriarch came before him, the king asked him: "I have killed Shamoun, the head of the Christians, and a large number of abbots and bishops. Why have you become the head of the people that I detest?" Shahdost replied: "The head of the Christians is the most High God. It is He who gives them the head of His choice. Just as the sea never runs short of water, Christianity will never perish from the Earth. The more Christians you kill, the more they will multiply."

Shapour was angered by these words and ordered him to be killed along with his companions. His execution was carried out at the same spot where Mar Shamoun had been put to death. This was on 20 February, 343 AD. His companions were also killed, who included. His followers collected their bodies and buried them in the church. Shahdost was patriarch for two years and five months.

7

Mar Youhanna of Arbeel and Father Yacoub

Youhanna was the bishop of Arbeel; he was nick-named the 'son of Maryam' (son of Mary). He was most devoted to prayer, meditation and the soul-inspiring worship of God. He desired to be martyred like his brothers and sisters before him. Often, tears leaked from his eyes and dripped down his cheeks whenever he remembered the people who were fortunate enough to be martyred for Jesus, while he felt he was not lucky enough to be so chosen. But he had patience, and would pray constantly to die a martyr for his faith, like others before him.

One evening, as he was praying fervently and beseeching the Lord to grant him martyrdom, he saw a young man with a glorious presence, with bright lights shining strongly from his face and holding a sword with a gold crown on it. He approached Youhanna and placed the crown on Youhanna's head, saying: "be glad, Youhanna, for what you have longed for and wanted from the bottom of your heart you will attain."

Youhanna woke up and realised that finally his prayers had been answered. Seven days later, he was captured and imprisoned on the orders of Damshahpor, the governor of Arbeel, along with Father Yacoub, who was nicknamed 'the ardent'.

After spending a year in prison they were taken to King Shahpor, who had them severely flogged, and told them to worship the sun so that they could gain their freedom back.

But Youhanna mocked the king for worshipping silent elements that were made for man, and asked the king to kill them as quickly as he could so that they would be free from their captivity and able to go on to their real home. When the king heard their replies, he wasted no time and killed them on the spot. This took place on 1 November, 344 AD.

8

Mar Abraham

braham succeeded Mar Youhanna as the priest of Arbeel (present day Irbil, northern Iraq), After holding his position for a short while, he was captured by the ruthless Adoorfer, the governor of Hedyabder.

Ardoofer subjected Abraham to heavy, relentless beatings and dreadful torture in order to make him worship the sun. But the devoted priest remained resolute in his beliefs and faith in Christ. When he was being tortured he would scream: "I only believe in the one God, and to Him I kneel, Him I worship and adore, and I will never renounce my true faith." The governor replied: "save yourself and do as your king commands, you miserable imbecile." Abraham replied: "I scorn you and your gods and have contempt for your king and his order, because he is trying to obscure the truth in dark shadows and disrespects my humility with his pride; but let him know that my humility will crush his pride."

The enraged governor ordered Abraham's beheading, and the saint was martyred in the village of Talneeh on the 5 February, 345 AD.

9

Mar Henannya al-Arbelee

ar Henannya was a well-known Christian resident of Arbeel (present day Erbil, northern Iraq). Because of his Christian faith he was captured, tortured and abused by its governor, Adoorshakh. In prison, he was subjected to daily beatings. One day, they pinned his body to the ground, and his torturers started bashing his body with hammers until most of his bones were broken. He endured all this painful torture without uttering a word or a scream, until he passed out and his seemingly dead body lay motionless on the prison floor. The guards thought that he was dead, and they dragged his body and dumped it in an open market for all to see. After the curious crowds had disappeared, some Christians managed to take his body to his house. Many of his followers and some priests arrived at his house to pay their respects for their murdered priest.

As they were praying for him, he suddenly opened his eyes and told them of the vision that had appeared to him. He said:

> Pray, brothers, to the just God who will punish our tormentors for what they have done to us, and who will reward us with eternal rest in His kingdom, for I saw a long ladder resting on Earth with its top reaching heaven, and the heavenly angels came down to take me to the top and they told me to be

brave and follow them. They told me that they will show me a place far greater and more beautiful than this earth.

Hearing what he said, his followers were startled. They knelt and started praying fervently until Henannya breathed his last breath and died. This occurred on December 12, 346 AD.

10

Mar Berhadsheba

erhadsheba was a deacon at a church in Erbil, northern Iraq. He was well known for his pious and austere living. He was imprisoned on the order of Damshahboor, governor of Erbil, in the 15th year of the 40 years of the Sassanids' persecution of the Christians.

In prison he was badly tortured and maimed. He was ordered by the governor to renounce his Christian faith, make offerings to the gods of water and fire and declare the sun as his god. But Berhadsheba laughed at the governor and said:

> What kind of hypocrite are you? You order me to abandon my true God and force me to worship your false Gods? How dare you try to tempt me from the righteous path that I have been on since my childhood until my old age and make me fall in the hateful trap of a pagan religion? I believe in the one true living God, whereas you worship silent beings; nothing will separate me from my love for Jesus, not you, your king or any amount of torture you want to inflict on me.

Hearing these words, Damshaboor exploded, rage and anger fighting within him, and his eyes became bloodshot. He felt ridiculed. He gave the order for Berhadsheba to be beheaded by another Christian, called Aaji, who had been imprisoned along with Berhadsheba. They were both

taken to a location near the village of Hazza. Berhadsheba
was bound and forced to kneel, and they gave Aaji a sword
to behead him. Aajai struck Berhadsheba seven times in
his neck, but each time he failed to kill him because his
hands were trembling from fear, and he dropped the
blood-stained sword to the ground. The guards yelled insults at Aaji and threatened to kill him instead of Berhadsheba. Aaji put his hands on his head, muttering an
incantation, and started praying for Berhadsheba with an
ardour that made his heart pound. Sweat mixed with tears
ran in rivulets down his face. He thrust his sword into
Berhadsheba's heart, killing him instantly.

Aaji was punished by God. After he had killed Berhadsheba, his right arm swelled up and the pain spread
throughout his body; he fell to the ground and died immediately. Two guards were left to keep people from taking the body of Berhadsheba away. The crowd and some
monks tried to bribe the guards to give them his body so
that they could bury it properly. No matter how hard they
tried, however, they failed to bribe the stubborn guards.
But eventually the restless crowd attacked the guards and
took the body for burial. The martyrdom of Mar Berhadsheba took place on 20 July, 356 AD.

11

Mar Qardagh

Qardagh was born in the village of Barhaptoon in northern Iraq around AD 325, to a noble and wealthy family. His father, Kooshnawi (a descendant of Assyrian kings), was dedicated to the Zoroastrian religion. He was a philanthropist who built many temples and donated generously to its priests.

From youth, Qardagh was a prodigious marksman, polo-player and hunter. He was heavily built; a tall and handsome figure with a deep, majestic voice. When King Shapour II visited his parents he was impressed by Qardagh's archery skills and athleticism; his precocious talents captured the imagination of the king. On the following morning of the visit, Qardagh joined the king's hunting entourage of three hundred noblemen and one hundred bodyguards. As they entered a dense forest they spotted two stags, and the king called for Qardagh to demonstrate his archery skills. The young man loosed his arrow with such speed and power that it went through both stags and killed them.

The king was lost in amazement. He showered Qardagh with many gifts and appointed him as a Marzipan, a government official, of the frontier region of Atour, an area stretching from present-day Irbil in northern Iraq to Nissibes in southern Turkey. This area bordered the Byzantine Empire, and Christianity had already spread there. The Christians were perturbed when they heard about his appointment because they were aware how zealous the new governor's family was in their devotion to the Zoroastrian religion.

Upon taking his post, Qardagh built many temples and commenced work on his castle, on a hill called Malgee. He completed the project within two years. Opposite the castle, he built a huge fire temple, and many priests were appointed to serve in it. As he was supervising the final touches to his castle, one night he saw a vision of a heavily armoured knight poking his spear at him; and the knight told him that he would die a martyr for Jesus in front of his castle. The knight was St George. Qardagh told his mother about his vision, and she warned him not to persecute the Christians, as, she said, their God is just.

In a cave nestled in Mount Safeen, overlooking Shaqlawa (51 km to the northeast of Erbil, northern Iraq), lived a monk by the name of Abdishu (to this day his cave still exists). One night during his prayers he heard a voice instructing him to leave his cave and seek out Qardagh, as he, Qardagh, wished to be converted to Christianity. As the monk headed to the castle, he came across a party of joyous men who were chatting excitedly; it was Qardagh and his friends heading to a field to play polo. Abdishu nonchalantly walked towards them and blocked their way. They were surprised at the hermit's bold impropriety and cussedness. The angry men jostled and battered the monk. He was dragged to the castle to be interrogated after they finished their game.

As they commenced their warm-up before the game, one of the players swiped the ball hard, but it did not move and remained still. Everyone took turns, and hit the ball with their mallets, but they were amazed that, no matter how much harder they hit the ball, it did not move. It

seemed nailed to the ground. Qardagh ordered one of his
men to dismount and to lift the ball and throw it away. His
friend lifted the ball and threw it as hard as he could, only
for it to fall at his feet. They were dumbfounded. One of
his companions pointed out that the monk they beat up
had drawn the sign of a cross and muttered something
with his lips; perhaps he had cast a spell on them?
Qardagh returned to his castle, gripped by a growing self-
righteous rage; he ordered Abdishu to be brought to him
for interrogation.

Qardagh questioned Abdishu about his identity, and
asked how he possessed such supernatural powers. He
yelped insults at the monk. The hermit endured his abuse
with humility and talked with gusto about Christianity and
Jesus. Qardagh realised that behind the hermit's servile,
weak exterior lay concealed a strong will-power. As the
monk was dragged to prison, Abdishu told Qardagh that
the following day he would witness another miracle. The
next day, Qardagh and his companions were out hunting.
Every time one of them loosed his arrows, they would fly
no further than their feet. Spontaneously, all of them drew
their bows fully and discharged their arrows as hard as they
could, only to see them fall on the ground. Their faces were
etched with incredulity and anxiety.

Qardagh realised that a miracle was unfolding before
his eyes, and he remembered the words of Abdishu. He
returned to his castle, overtaken by anxiety and fear, and
decided to free the monk, unaware that, during the night,
an angel of the Lord had appeared to Abdishu and already
released him from his cell. As the guards went to get him,
to their astonishment they saw the jail door open and his
shackles on the floor. The terrified guards rushed back and
informed Qardagh of the monk's disappearance.

Qardagh withdrew to his private quarters. Alone in his room, he realised that the God of the Christians is truly great. He subconsciously drew the sign of the cross on the wall of his room. From this moment, a great change occurred in his life: he felt pure, as if his soul was cleansed by his new faith. Qardagh started praying, ruefully, and he implored the God of the Christians to let him see Abdishu and ask for forgiveness, and for the monk to teach him about the Christian faith. During the night, he saw a vision of the monk telling him how to get to his mountain cave.

In the morning, Qardagh disguised himself, took two of his loyal men, and headed to the mountain cave of Abdishu. After several days riding, they reached the cave, and were greeted by the monk. Qardagh dismounted swiftly and knelt on the ground before Abdishu and asked for his forgiveness. The pious monk helped him stand on his feet, embraced him warmly, and took him inside his cave. His companions took Qardagh's horse to the nearby monastery of Sapparyashu, where they stayed overnight. Abdishu started teaching Qardagh how to pray and meditate.

In a cave nine miles north of Abdishu's mountain dwelled a monk by the name of Booya. He lived a strict ascetic life, and had never ventured outside his cave for almost sixty-eight years. This cave still exists in northern Iraq, and the Christian locals of Shaqlawa still celebrate the monk's feast day on the third Monday after Easter. Booya had a vision to visit the cave of Abdishu and help him guide the newly converted Qardagh.

Abdishu was astonished when he saw the old monk in his cave. The two of them embraced each other warmly; they were filled with joy at Qardagh's conversion to Christianity. Booya hugged Qardagh and spoke to him about Jesus and the Christian religion. The three of them spent some time in prayer and meditation. Then the old monk embraced the two and returned to his cave. Qardagh spent a further five days with Abdishu, and asked Abdishu to baptise him. Abdishu took Qardagh to the monastery of Sapparyashu, along with his two loyal companions, and they were all baptised in a joyful ceremony. After spending another week with Abdishu, Qardagh returned to his castle immersed in joy and happiness.

When Qardagh reached his castle, he immediately asked for a monk by the name of Isaac, a renowned friar who roamed the area. Isaac taught Qardagh the psalms and explained the Bible to him. Qardagh abandoned all frivolous things, and stopped eating meat. He withdrew from society and devoted himself to the purpose of spiritual renewal and a return to God. He started giving alms to the poor and to the orphans living in monasteries in his area. These acts disturbed his family and relatives, especially his father, a wealthy landlord, who was perturbed at his son's squandering of his land and possessions. It was bad enough for Qardagh to convert to Christianity; it was even worse that he was giving away all the wealth that they had accumulated. Qardagh's wife, Shushan, wrote to her father and complained about his actions.

After two years, Qardagh decided to re-visit his mentor Abdishu. The monk was delighted to see him, and they went to meet monk Booya again. Qardagh stayed with the two holy men for over a month, enjoying the rustic beauty and peacefulness of the area.

News of Qardagh's conversion to Christianity and his lack of interest in warfare reached his enemies. During his stay with the monks, a raiding party of Romans and Arabs attacked his castle. Many of his knights were killed, and the invaders took captive his parents, his wife and his relatives together with a large booty. Two hundred and thirty-five of his bravest knights survived the battle and

headed for the cave of Abdishu. Qardagh was surprised to
see their gloomy faces. He laughed at them and asked why
they looked so petrified; it was, he said, as though they
had just escaped their deaths. Churning with anger, one
of his knights said, "what do you expect when our commander and governor dwells in a cave with thieves and
sorcerers?" Immediately on finishing his sentence the
knight fell to the ground and breathed no more. His companions were astonished when they saw their brave friend
dead, killed for uttering a few words, and they all asked to
be baptised and converted to Christianity.

Qardagh decided to save his family and recover his possessions. With the blessing of Booya and Abdishu he gathered his remaining knights and returned to his castle. He
was saddened to see the devastation inflicted on his land,
but with Christianity etched on his heart he decided to
forgive his enemies and not seek revenge. He dispatched
his brother with a message to the raiders to return what
belonged to him. His wife had been very clever; she had
left some traces of her clothes as clues that would lead to
their whereabouts.

But the raiders decapitated his brother and returned
his head to Qardagh. Incandescent with rage, he gathered
his knights and prepared for battle. He and his men spent
some time praying in the church, and with his hands
raised to his head he muttered an incantation and started
praying. He vowed that if he were to be victorious in his
battle all the temples of fire would be demolished in his
region. They headed for battle; Qardagh was wearing a
large, luminous cross on his chest.

He met his enemies by the mountain of Qardoo. They
were drinking, and their laughter resounded through the
mountains. As the darkness of night was receding, heralding a new morning, Qardagh and his men attacked their

camp. Their attack was so furious and so swift that within one hour the battle was over and almost all of his enemies had been killed, or drowned in the Khabour River. This battle took place in AD 356 near the village of Beedar, west of Zakho (300 miles northwest of Baghdad).

Qardagh returned triumphant; he had regained his wife, his parents and all his possessions. He was in an ebullient mood. He replaced all temples of fire with churches, fulfilling his vow. He even converted the temple built by his father, in honour of Qardagh's birth, in the village of Barhaptoon to a monastery. The Zoroastrian priests and their chief, Mudban Moobedheard, were outraged by his actions and complained bitterly to the king.

The king loved Qardagh and admired his bravery in battle; he was fascinated with his daring attack that had left thousands of his enemies dead. He dismissed the priests' complaints. All of the head priests then produced more witnesses and lodged an appeal to the king to investigate the matter. The king succumbed to their pressure and summoned Qardagh for questioning.

At their meeting Qardagh confessed to the king about his conversion to Christianity. The king asked him to renounce his new faith and return to his Zoroastrian beliefs. By doing so he would be rewarded handsomely. But Qardagh clung obstinately to his new faith. His case was put before the notorious chief inquisitor, Shaherkhwast, a ruthless and delusional judge responsible for punishing all those who converted to Christianity. Shaherkhwast also ordered Qardagh to renounce his new faith; if he did, he would be spared torture. But instead Qardagh started praying loudly. Shaherkhwast grew increasingly vituperative the more Qardagh prayed. The inquisitor's eyes were glinting with rage. If it were not for the king's orders, he would have killed Qardagh at once. Qardagh was shackled and escorted back to his own castle. As he approached it, Qardagh broke down and wept, sank to his knees and prayed to Jesus to unshackle him. All of a sudden his shackles turned and unfastened. His captors were startled and ran in fright.

Qardagh entered the castle and shut the gate, preparing to fight alongside his loyal knights. They started shooting arrows at his captors, killing most of them. A larger force was sent to retake his castle, but Qardagh defeated them. The king summoned Qardagh's elder tribesmen and asked them to intervene and negotiate a peaceful settlement of the affair, but they failed.

During his sleep, Qardagh saw a dream of a man being stoned with pearls. When he woke up in the morning he asked monk Isaac to interpret his dream. The monk told him that this was St Stephen, the first Christian martyr. Isaac read St Stephen's story to Qardagh from the Acts of the Apostles. Qardagh realised that his hour had come. He made the sign of the cross and ordered the gates to be opened. His companions clung on to him, begging him to stay, but to no avail. He walked slowly towards his enemies.

Everyone gathered around him, with vulgar jests and insulting sneers passing from lip to lip, like the bellowing of wild beasts. The crowd could contain their anger no longer. Then, a torrent of stones. As he was being pelted by the mob, Qardagh seemed oblivious to them and continued with his prayers; and he drew the sign of the cross on his forehead. He prayed that the Lord would receive his spirit, and that his killers would be forgiven. He was pelted with larger stones, and despite the agony that racked his frame he continued with his prayers. He felt his pulse race and the moisture evaporate from his mouth.

As the last gleam of light was fading from his eyes, Qardagh cried out, "I will only die if my father stones me."

His father heard his cry; he took a large stone and, with his eyes closed, dropped it on his son's head. Qardagh died instantly, on a Friday, AD 358. His feast day is still celebrated by the Christians of Iraq on 23 August.

12

Mar Behnam and his sister Sarah

When the Emperor Constantius II died in 361 AD he named his last surviving cousin, Julian, as his successor. He was the last non-Christian ruler of the Roman Empire, and it was his desire to bring the empire back to its ancient Roman values in order to save it from dissolution, as he saw it. Julian attempted to revive traditional pagan Roman religious practices at the expense of Christianity. His anti-Christian sentiment and promotion of Neoplatonic paganism caused him to be remembered as Julian the Apostate (a person who has abandoned their religious principles). Julian ordered Christians to convert to the religion of the state or face lashing and beheading.

Fear gripped the hearts of the Christians residing in Amed, present day Diyarbakir, in south-east Turkey. They gathered at the monastery of Zekneen, where they agreed to stand firm and die in the name of Jesus Christ rather than convert to paganism. Word of their stance reached the governor, and he wrote to Julian and asked for his help to quash the large number of Christians who refused to reject their religion. Julian sent an army to Amed and killed hundreds of Christians; some managed to flee and re-settle elsewhere.

Among the men who survived the massacre was Mar Mattie, a holy man from Abgershad, near Amed. He was well known for performing miracles and for his healing power. Mar Mattie, his followers, and some monks travelled southwards towards Nineveh in Iraq, and settled on a mountain 3,400 feet above sea level. They built a small church and continued in their worship. For many years they lived in peace and tranquillity, but news of Mar Mattie's healing power and his miraculous acts reached King Sanharib (Sennacherib) II, the governor of Nineveh in northern Iraq, during the reign of Shapour II. Much like Julian the Apostate, Sanharib disliked Christianity; he was greatly influenced by the Persian Zoroastrian religion. The king had two children: a son called Behnam and a daughter by the name of Sarah, who suffered from leprosy at a young age. The king summoned some Christians to tell him about Mar Mattie, but they denied his existence, as they feared for his life.

Behnam and forty of his companions went out on a hunting trip near the mountain where Mattie lived. They came across a wild deer, and they chased after it until they decided to retire at sundown. During the night, an angel appeared to Behnam and said to him, "awaken young man." Behnam was frightened, and asked the angel who he was, but the angel said to him, "don't be afraid, I am an angel of God and I was sent to guide you to the righteous path; you have been chosen to be an instrument of God and you will perform great miracles." Behnam asked how and when this would happen. The angel replied, "on this mountain lives a saint who will teach you God's word and show you the right faith. Find him and listen to his teaching."

In the morning, Behnam called his companions and told them what he had seen. Among them was a Christian who knew about Mar Mattie; he told Behnam how Mar

Mattie had saved and healed many sick people with his prayers. Behnam gathered some of his men and climbed the mountain to find Mar Mattie. God led their steps to the cave where Mar Mattie lived, and when Mar Mattie saw the climbers he was moved by the Holy Spirit and went to meet them. When he noticed that they were from the royal court, he asked them what they were doing in such a remote place. Behnam told Mar Mattie about his dream and what the angel had told him. Mar Mattie was convinced that this was the hand of God at work, and started to tell Behnam about the Christian religion and how God's only son died and rose from the dead on the third day to save humanity.

Behnam believed everything Mar Mattie told him, yet he wanted to see the wonder of God in real life, so he told Mar Mattie about his sick sister and asked Mar Mattie to accompany him to the city to heal her. But Mar Mattie asked Behnam instead to bring his sister to him, and that he would pray for her. When Behnam returned home from his trip he went to see his mother and sister. He confided in his mother what had happened to him during his hunting trip, and asked her to allow him to take his sister to Mar Mattie to heal her.

The following morning, Behnam took his sister to the cave. When they arrived, Mar Mattie knelt down, lifted his eyes to heaven and prayed to God to heal Sarah. He then struck the ground with his stick, and instantly a spring of water burst from the earth. Mar Mattie turned to Sarah and asked her to repent her sins and believe in Jesus so that she would be healed and her spirit would be pure. Sarah renounced the devil and the pagan religion and believed in God, His Son and the Holy Spirit. Mar Mattie baptised Sarah: he drew the sign of the cross on her forehead and Sarah emerged from the water healed and inspired. When Behnam and his forty companions witnessed this miracle, they also asked to be baptised. However, Mar Mattie told them that very soon they would be united with Jesus. He prophesised their martyrdom.

When King Sanharib saw his cured daughter, an unfathomable surge of joy almost took his breath away. He asked Sarah about what had happened to her. She told him that she had been cured by God, the creator of heaven and earth, through his servant Mar Mattie. Her reply angered the king, and he warned her not to speak foolishly. However, Sarah told him that she and Behnam had been baptised and would only worship the God who cured her, not the dumb stone idols, and said how they wished that their father would follow in their footsteps.

The city was abuzz with news of the king's children's and their companions' conversion to Christianity. The people of Nineveh were dismayed, and a surge of anger welled up inside them, which alarmed the king. He called his advisers and noblemen and asked for their opinion on how to handle his children's situation, as he was hesitant to kill them. They advised the king to persuade them gently and to offer them more privileges and wealth if they decided to renounce Christianity.

Behnam fervently told his father that they would not worship some stone gods made by human hands and worshipped by fools. Sarah added: "How can you fail to see the transformation in me after I was healed from my illness? You are proving to be more stupid than your stone idols, because they have no brains, but you are wilfully refusing to see the truth. I reject you and condemn your brainless gods and will follow the teachings of Jesus Christ." The king seethed with frustration at the defiance of his children. The ferocity of their wishes shocked him, but there was nothing he could do to stem it.

The following day, King Sanahrib called his noblemen again and consulted with them about a suitable punishment for his stubborn children. They advised him to announce a feast day in the city, and present the pagan gods with offerings and sacrifices in front of the crowds and invite his children to the feast, and ask them to kneel before the gods. When Behnam and Sarah arrived at the feast, their father welcomed them with great respect and affection and asked them to present prayers and sacrifices to the gods in accordance with the pagan custom.

Both children remained faithful to Jesus and refused to comply with their father's request. The king, reeling from the humiliation, ordered his children to be imprisoned and killed. During the night, Behnam, Sarah and the forty companions who had been baptised with them, managed to escape. The news of the breakout reached the king, and he immediately ordered his soldiers to intercept them. He gave the soldiers strict orders to kill all of escapees, including his own children, and to show no mercy. The soldiers caught up with them near a hill in Nimrud, and then the slaughter began.

The soldiers held Behnam and Sarah and made them watch the killing. They started hacking everyone. Heads and body parts were flying in the air; rivulets of blood ran through the earth. The soldiers were unmoved by the waves of cries and screams. Behnam and Sarah were distraught, and their eyes were aghast, for they saw the anguish of their companions. After the killing had stopped, the soldiers asked Behnam and Sarah for the last time to renounce their Christianity, but they refused. Behnam asked the soldiers to give them some time to pray before they killed them. The soldiers obeyed and acquiesced to his request. With a fervent intensity and warmth of spirit, Behnam and Sarah held hands together; looking up at the sky, and prayed silently. When they were ready they asked the soldiers to carry out their orders. This took place on 10 December, 372 AD.

As the soldiers were preparing the bodies to be burned, the earth trembled and opened up, swallowing all the bodies. On their return, the soldiers told the king of what had happened; he claimed a victory for the pagan gods, who had buried the bodies deep inside the dark earth so that they would never be seen anymore.

A few days after the killing of his children, the king's body was possessed by an evil spirit that tormented him; he spent days crying, screaming, tearing his clothes, gnashing his teeth and biting his body. The queen was in agony about her husband's situation. One day, she saw a vision of an angel saying: "Don't worry, your majesty, the king will be healed soon. Reject pagan worship of idols and take your husband to the spot where your children were killed, and you will both be saved and the king will be healed."

In the morning, the queen, escorted by soldiers, took the king to the location where the bodies of their children had been swallowed by the earth, and set camp. She prayed during the night and pleaded with her son to forgive them all, and to have mercy on his father and heal his sickness so that they might also believe in Jesus and join their children in their faith. Behnam appeared to his mother during her sleep and told her to call Mar Mattie, saying that he would cure his father. The queen returned to the city and sent word to Mar Mattie to visit her. He obeyed her request and made his way to the city, along with some monks, passing by the spot where the children had been killed.

The queen warm-heartedly welcomed Mar Mattie and explained to him what had befallen them since the killing of their children. Mar Mattie started preaching to her about the Holy Scriptures until she believed. He prayed and beseeched God to heal the king; he then turned to Sanharib and performed an exorcism on him and uttered loudly the name of Jesus Christ. The demon left the king's body, screaming like a wild beast and cursing Jesus of Nazareth and his followers for humiliating him on Earth. Both the king and the queen now believed in Jesus Christ and were baptised. Eventually the whole city converted to Christianity and many sick people were healed.

After his recovery, the king offered Mar Mattie wealth, and he even told him that he would give him half of his kingdom, should he ask for it. But Mar Mattie refused the king's money and only asked for a monastery to be built for his faithful. The king built a great monastery for Mar Mattie, on the same spot where his daughter had been cured. Many people would come from faraway places to live near the monastery or in the nearby caves. Eventually, the number of people living in and around the monastery reached over seven thousand. Hence, the mountain was called Alfaf, meaning 'thousands'. Mar Mattie placed the relics of Behnam and his sister in it.

When the king decided to build a monument to honour his martyred children and their companions, the queen asked him to involve her in this project as a way of doing her penance. Behnam appeared to the queen in a vision and told her to send two pious men from the monastery of Mar Mattie who were worthy of moving their relics to the monument. The task fell to Mar Ibrahim, the deputy of Mar Zakka (who succeeded Mar Mattie as head of the monastery after his death). Mar Ibrahim was accompanied by two monks to help him with his task.

When the party reached the location of the killing, to their amazement they saw bodies scattered on the ground. There was a beautiful fragrance coming from the bodies.

The queen identified the bodies of Behnam and Sarah among them. The bodies were removed to a suitable burial place, and the bodies of Behnam and Sarah were placed in the mausoleum, where their mother erected two marble columns for them. Mar Ibrahim returned to his monastery after his work was completed, but not before the queen had pleaded with him to take as much gold and silver as he needed to build a monastery in his name. This was built in Kokyatha, meaning 'storms', to the north of the monastery of Mar Mattie.

The two monks who helped Ibrahim to build the mausoleum remained behind to pray and help the visitors and the sick who visited the relics of the saints and asked to be cured. After a while, the two monks grew weary of the living conditions and the sheer number of visitors they had to look after. God sent them a solution in the shape of a devout man. Isaac was a wealthy Persian merchant on his way to the Holy Land for a pilgrimage. He was accompanied by a number of people from his household, his guards and his servants. Among his servants was a man whom Isaac loved dearly, but who was possessed by an evil spirit that knocked him about and made him suffer bitterly. Isaac pitied the monk's living conditions.

The monks told him about the story of Behnam and Sarah and the healing power of their relics. Isaac went to a secluded place and prayed for his servant to be cured. Behnam appeared to Isaac in a dream and said to him that his prayers had been answered and his servant would be cured. As a sign of gratitude, he was told to build a monastery where his servant would be healed. Isaac woke up and told the monks about his dream. They prayed to the relics for guidance and for healing. The following night, Isaac's servant saw Behnam in his dream; he appeared in the shape of a soldier with a long spear, and he pierced the servant's body, shouting "may you be healed in the name of Jesus." Instantly the bad spirit left the servant's body in the shape of a pig. The servant emitted a loud squeal and awoke the others and his master. They questioned him about what had disturbed him, and they were amazed by the account of his dream and the miracle that had taken place.

Isaac told the monks about what had happened to his servant and his intention to build a monastery as instructed by Behnam in his dream. The monks sent word to Mar Zakka, who was overjoyed and sent his deputy Mar Ibrahim and some helpers to build the monastery. As they were about to lay the corner stone of the monastery, Behnam appeared in a vision to Mar Ibrahim and told him not to lay the stone by the well but at a distance from it. A large monastery was built, with living quarters for the sick.

Mar Behnam and his sister Sarah are honoured on 10 December by both the Syriac Orthodox and Syriac Catholic churches. He is also considered a martyr and a saint by both the Assyrian Church of the East and the Chaldean Church.

13

Father Yacoub and Deacon Azzad

acoub was a priest in the village of Esfargalta, and Azzad a deacon in Bate Negar in the Plains of Hedyab (Belad Hedyab, northern Iraq). They were informed upon to Khorsheed, the governor of Hedyab, who put them in prison in Arbeel (present day Erbil, northern Iraq). They were tortured in an abominable manner for 6 months, such as by having sand mixed with vinegar poured in their nostrils, and by being kept naked outside in the freezing snow.

Every day they were tortured in a different way and told that if they worshipped the sun and fire their lives would be spared. But they refused to obey the governor. At one stage, he asked them to swallow blood from a sacrifice, and also to get married; if they did, he would free them. Yacoub was the stronger of the two, and replied: "you and your followers devour blood, for you are defiled dogs who enjoy barking at people, while we are innocents and pure people who do not drink blood, and the more you make us suffer the greater our glory will be in heaven." A sudden surge of anger welled up inside the governor, and he cursed Yacoub and ordered his guards to beat them with thorny sticks, and then they were thrown into a small, dark prison cell.

During that night, Yacoub saw a dream: his sister, who was a nun, entering the cell; she wrapped his hands, feet and his head with silk sheets and dressed him in white clothes. This was the ritual carried out before burying corpses. In the morning, Yacoub told Azzad about his dream, and encouraged him to be strong and prepared to die for Jesus, because He was inviting them to join Him at His heavenly feast.

On the morning of 14 April, 374, they both started praying in readiness, and at around 3pm they were taken out of the city walls and beheaded. Their corpses were guarded by soldiers to prevent the Christians from taking them for a burial. During the night, two bright rays were seen shining from heaven straight down on the spot where their heads were. This happened for two more nights. But as their bodies could not be removed, the wild dogs devoured them.

14

Mar Eethallaha al-Nohadri

etter for me to die and attain eternal life than live and be dead forever. These words were uttered more than 17 centuries ago by a brave deacon, while enduring terrible torture at the hands of the Persian governor, Etherker Kasheed, because he believed in one God and in Jesus Christ. His name was Eethallaha al No-hadri, a deacon at the church of Nohadra (present day Duhok, northern Iraq).

Eethallaha, (literally meaning there is God) was a sincere and intense man dedicated to the love of God. He was born in Nohadra around 315 AD. It is likely that he was called Eethallaha after his martyrdom because of his strong commitment to the Christian faith and his refusal to obey the pagan Persian rulers who governed his region. His torturers inflicted a cruel and hideous punishment upon him, all intended so that he would renounce his Christianity, but the valiant deacon refused to do so; in his suffering he cried out loudly, "there is God." Hence, he was known by that name. After his martyrdom many Christians were named after him, especially church deacons.

In the year 376 AD, King Shapour II encouraged his governors to increase the severity of their repressive measures and carry out the killing of all the Christians in their districts. In the valley of Rawanduz, Eethallaha, together with an 80-year-old priest, Akbeshma, and a 70-year-old priest, Yousif, were detained. They were tied up and brought for questioning to the city of Erbil and dragged before its governor, Etherker Kasheed.

After the three men had been questioned and tortured, the governor ordered Eethallaha to kneel and worship the sun as his new god. The governor also ordered him to drink sacrificial blood, and to marry in order to save his own life and spare himself the pain and torture he was destined to suffer. Upon hearing this, Eethallaha screamed his famous words, "better for me to die and attain eternal life than to live and be dead forever." The three faithful men endured severe torture until Father Akbesham lost his life. The governor decided that the best way to humiliate and kill the remaining two was to gather a large crowd of Christians from their native villages and force them to stone them to death.

Father Yousif was taken to the outskirts of Erbil to be stoned. His body was guarded for three days so that it could not be buried according to the Christian rituals. On the fourth day, a severe thunderstorm broke out with a strong, cold wind. Fear spread among the guards, and in the ensuing chaotic weather conditions the corpse of the priest disappeared from view, never to be seen ever again. Eethallaha was taken to his village of Nohadra, where he was tied to a wooden pole and stoned to death by a crowd of Christian men and women who had been forcibly led to the hill for the stoning. His corpse was guarded for two nights, but on the third night it was stolen by loyal Christians and buried according to their custom.

Miraculously, a tree rapidly grew out from the spot where Eethallaha was stoned, and was henceforth a source of blessings for the people of the area. After five years, the tree was pulled out by spiteful people; where it stood, eye witnesses said they saw bands of angels sweeping up and around at night, blessing God.

15

Mar Abed al-Maseeh

In 390 AD, Zoroastrianism was the dominant religion in the Persian Empire and Judaism was practiced openly, without fear of persecution. In Sinjar, northwest Iraq, there was a wealthy Jew who owned a large number of cattle and was the head of the Jewish community; his name was Lahwey (Levi). He was very careful and strict with his wealth and cattle and did not trust anyone with his assets unless they were from his own family and household. That is why he divided the herding of the cattle between his sons, including his youngest son Asheer (Abed al-Maseeh).

When Asheer was 11 years old, his father put him in charge of a herd of cows, which he would take out from morning until night to graze and drink water from a nearby stream. While at the stream, he would meet other young boys, Christians and pagans, playing together. However, during lunchtime, all the boys would separate from each other and would eat food only with those of the same religion. Asheer ate alone, as he was the only Jew in the group.

Asheer preferred to eat his meal with the Christian group if he could, and normally they allowed him to be with them; they told him stories about Jesus and his disciples and suggested to him that he should be baptised and convert to Christianity. However, on one occasion as the boys were gathered for their usual lunch break and Asheer

came to join them they refused his company unless he was
baptised in the name of Jesus. He replied: "here is the
water; I agree to be baptised." But his friends told him that
he must be baptised by a priest. Asheer said:

> You are right, but there are no priests here and the
> church is a long way away. Also, I am afraid of my
> family; if they hear I have been converted at your
> hands they will not allow me to enjoy your com-
> pany and my baptism will be of no consequence.
> In any case, I am sure that Christ can see I have a
> willing mind and a heart set on being one of you;
> surely a simple ceremony is preferable to Him than
> a big celebration—make the best of this opportu-
> nity so you will be rewarded by Him.

The group agreed that this was an opportune moment to
bring this lost lamb back into Christ's fold and they immersed him in water, baptising him in the name of the Father and the Son and the Holy Spirit. They prayed in the
name of Jesus to make the water holy for the baptism. He
was immersed in the water three times and was pro-
nounced Christian. The called him Abed al-Maseeh ('Servant of Jesus'), clothed him in their finest garments, and
carried him on their shoulders to celebrate the event, just
like a priest would carry a newly baptised child. Afterwards
they sat together to eat, with all their attention focused on
him. Suddenly, a beautiful aroma arose from the group
which spread in the air and reached the pagan boys who
had been watching the events unfold with amazement.

The Christian friends of Abed al-Maseeh encouraged
and motivated him to value and respect what he had chosen and not to go back to his Jewish beliefs or keep his
baptism a secret; in return he promised his friends that
they would be proud of him. One of the boys said:

As you all know it is not a Jewish custom to pierce the ear of a male, so let's pierce Abdel al-Maseeh's ear and give him a golden earring as a sign of our love and as a sign of his solid determination to become a true Christian and renounce Judaism until the end.

They all agreed and put the idea into action.

When Abed al-Maseeh returned home wearing the gold earring, his mother noticed it and flew into a rage of disapproval. She was beside herself with worry and asked him:

What have you done, my son; what is that in your ear? Who tricked you into bringing this shame on our family, which no doubt will be severely punished? Don't you know that the Law of Moses clearly states that a male's ear must not be pierced unless he is enslaved to his master forever? Your father is very strict with the law; if he were to see your ear—and it is very hard to hide the ear—what will he do to you?

Abed al-Maseeh replied:

Be calm, mother, and don't be so frightened; from now on I am a Christian and a slave to Jesus; I have loved him and He is my master and God. As for the law of Moses, it does not forbid a slave to love his master; on the contrary, it states that a slave's ear should be pierced at his master's house so that he serve him forever, and I have achieved that now; my ear was pierced at baptism so that I will be the slave of Jesus forever, a promise I intend to keep as long as I live.

His mother was bewildered at his reply and wondered who had converted her son to Christianity. Abed al-

Maseeh told her all about Jesus, which touched her
deeply; she saw in him a divine holiness and beauty, and
she could smell a heavenly scent emanating from his body,
which made her believe that the work of God had been
performed within her son. For the next thirty days, his
mother was careful to keep him away from his father, as
she knew that her husband would kill his son for greatly
embarrassing him among his Jewish clan. As for Abed al-
Maseeh, he would leave in the mornings to herd the cows
and return in the evenings to his mother without his father
noticing, as he was preoccupied with his affairs.

Abed al-Maseeh heard from his friends the story of the
martyrdom of Babola and his three companions; his heart
was filled with a longing to receive the crown of martyrdom because of his faith in Jesus. While lying sleepless one
night, thinking about this story, he saw himself captive in
a dark dungeon in a sorry state and in agony along with
some other people. While sighing in the dark at this story,
he immediately saw a vision of a fine nobleman who struck
the ground with his heel, breaking it into two; he extended
his hand to Abed al-Maseeh and carried him up and
placed him among a group of people who then surrounded and worshipped the nobleman. Abed al-Maseeh's
fear disappeared and he fell on his knees and asked the
nobleman about his identity, and thanked him for saving
him from the dungeon.

The nobleman said:

> I am Jesus, and you had faith in me. Be brave and
> don't be afraid, as your place has been made ready
> for you and your crown of martyrdom is kept for
> you among the saints. Soon you will join me in
> heaven, because from the day you wore the earring
> and committed yourself to me at your baptism I in-
> tended to give you eternal life.

Hearing these words, Abed al-Maseeh was amazed and cried out: "Mercy and thanks to you, my God. If you wish, please tell me who were those tortured souls with me in the dungeon? They are stuck inside, unable to escape." Jesus said: "those are your people and fellow Jews from your father's clan; they are the ones who crucified me on the cross."

His mother heard him talking in his sleep, and she woke him up and asked him about his conversation. Abed al-Maseeh was still shaking from the excitement of seeing Jesus in his dream and he told his mother what he saw, and so she asked him to describe Jesus. He said:

> Jesus was wearing a torn garment showing his pierced side and scratched feet and hands; despite His bloody appearance he looked meek, and a bright light was shining from His face like a fire. On His attire was written: "this is the One who was crucified by the Jews in Jerusalem, but He intends to rescue the race of Adam from their sins; this is the Lamb of God who takes away the sins of the world; this is the One who will strive for the martyrs in the battle and crown them after they win."

He continued:

> I also saw young men about my age surrounding him and chanting: "God save me, God rescue me, blessed is He who comes in the name of the Lord"; some of the men were wearing bright sparkling crowns and carried olive branches, while others were carrying a gold bowl and presenting blood from their necks in communion, chanting: "this is our God, for whom we await; let us be happy and celebrate his salvation".

Abed al-Maseeh told his mother that he wanted to be among the men chanting to Jesus. This vision captured his heart and he did not wish to live after this day; he looked forward to death so that he would become closer to Jesus and the crowd surrounding him.

His mother was scared and heartbroken for him; she feared that his father would kill him if he heard of his dream. She tried to convince him that dreams have different meanings depending on how you interpret them, and not to pay much attention to it, but Abed al-Maseeh refused to listen to her argument; he insisted that the vision he saw was clear and direct, and that he must die for Jesus. He begged her to tell his family of his new faith and his death in Jesus' name. She agreed, but begged him to keep the matter between the two of them, otherwise his father and brothers would kill both of them. He obeyed his mother.

The next morning, he bid his mother farewell as he set off on his daily work to herd his cows. While he was on his way, Abed al-Maseeh saw an old man in the distance; and, as he got closer, he kneeled in front of the man and asked him to bless and baptise him. The man was surprised that he was recognised as a priest, because he was dressed in a traveller's outfit, and so asked Abed al-Maseeh how he knew that he was a priest. Abed al-Maseeh replied that he knew that God had inspired the priest to come and find him. The priest was amazed at what he heard, and told him that he was out searching for the one who was to be blessed before he received the crown of martyrdom. The priest blessed Abed al-Maseeh and asked the Holy Spirit to help him endure the pains of Christ. This took place on Friday, the day before the Jewish Sabbath. Abed al-Maseeh's father had organised a large banquet for all his friends and family, and sent his servants to bring all his sons to the feast. Abed al-Maseeh was brought to the banquet by these servants before he had the chance to escape and disappear into his mother's house.

When his father and his guests saw him, they noticed his earring; they were puzzled, and his father asked him angrily to explain who had deceived him into wearing what slaves would wear and shame the family in such a manner. Abed al-Maseeh replied: "do not worry, old man; I was not deceived, but I have become a slave for Jesus, and to show my commitment I am wearing the earring." Hearing this reply, his father went into a wild rage and slapped his son. He threw him on the floor and started kicking him relentlessly. The guests tried to restrain his father and asked him to leave the foolish boy alone and allow him to celebrate the Jewish feast. Then they tried to entice Abed al-Maseeh to eat with them, but he refused. This further embarrassed his father, who started to hit him again. The guests held him back, and again asked Abed al-Maseeh to eat with them on this great feast, for the sake of his father. But Abed al-Maseeh refused again.

The guests asked him to explain his behaviour so that they could understand what had changed him. Instead, he told them to repent for the sin of their ancestors, crucifying the Lamb of God whose coming John the Baptist proclaimed, and who John baptised in the River Jordan; he told them that he had been baptised in His name and wished to die for Him, and that unless they lifted the darkness from their eyes and believed and received baptism then they were as guilty as their ancestors.

This enraged the guests and his father, who picked a knife from a table and gave chase to his son to kill him. The future saint ran away, followed by his father, until the older man was out of breath and they had reached the river where Abed al-Maseeh had been baptised. It was nearly sunset and the start of the Jewish Sabbath; he now beseeched his father to calm down and not break the Sabbath by killing him, nor to stain his hands with the blood of Christ's servant. He said this not because he was afraid to die, but because he did not want his father to commit a deadly sin. However, his father kept chasing him.

As he reached another stream, Abed al-Maseeh again stopped, and started praying. He lifted his head to the sky, tears streaming down his face, and prayed to Jesus to forgive his father for the crime he was about to commit, and to have pity on his mother and to guard his brothers and friends. While he was praying, his father managed to catch up with him; he dragged him and stabbed him repeatedly until he died. This was on Friday 27 July, 390 AD. His father returned home that night and told his household that the knife in his hand was stained with their brother's blood. His mother was devastated by the loss of her son, but was also encouraged that if she were to die as a Christian then she would have the chance to see her son again in the afterlife. She longed to be baptised like her son, which soon happened near to where her son was killed.

The next day, Abed al-Maseeh's friends arrived at the stream, and they were horrified to see his slain body covered in blood. They wrapped him in fresh clothes and buried him, and they placed the blood-stained stone on his grave. They agreed not to tell anyone of their actions, as they were afraid they would be blamed for his death. Every day they would visit the burial spot and pray for their friend.

Shortly after this event, a caravan of merchants was travelling during the night on the road near Abed al-Maseeh's burial place. They noticed a powerful light shining in the distance. Some of the more curious of them walked closer to the spot and saw flames of fire coming out of the stone as bright as the sun and a heavenly smell filling the air. Because the merchants were Christian, they had no doubt that a miracle was taking place. They removed the stone that covered the grave and saw the body of a young man covered in blood; they believed he had been martyred, and took his body and the bloodied soil with them on their travels. When they rejoined the rest of the caravan they noticed that the flames followed them. A wealthy merchant by the name of Nasteer was travelling with the caravan. His wife was barren; when he realised that a miracle was taking place he swore that if his wife became pregnant, he would find out all about this dead person and name his child after him. He pledged to build a shrine from his own money and personally guard it and be the saint's servant for the rest of his life.

As for Abed al-Maseeh's friends, when they came to the stream, as was their habit, and noticed that the stone had been moved and the grave was now empty but for some blood-soaked soil, they cried bitterly and lamented their loss. Word spread that Abed al-Maseeh had been martyred at the hands of his father, and people gathered around the grave to pray. They saw the stone covered in red and a pierced ear with an earring. They created a shrine to their friend around the stone and put a sign that read: "Here lies the martyr Abed al-Maseeh." Many sick people visited the shrine and were cured of their illness, and the news soon spread all over the region of the miracles that were taking place at the grave.

When Nasteer arrived at his home he immediately started building his shrine, and placed Abed al-Maseeh's remains inside it. He told his household about what had happened on his travels and the promise he had made. His entire household would then pray daily around the shrine and ask for a miracle. Their prayers were answered, and the merchant's wife became pregnant. The family were overjoyed as a result of the miracle, and prayed constantly to God to reveal Abed al-Maseeh's name to them.

A year later, Nasteer was again travelling with his caravan. He stopped and walked up to the same spot where he had seen the light. To his amazement, he saw the small shrine which had been built for Abed al-Maseeh; inside it he saw a cross placed on top of a blood-stained stone. He understood from the people visiting it the story of Abed al-Maseeh. He told the people how his caravan had come across the grave and taken the body with them to their own land. The devout people begged Nasteer to bring back to them some of the relics of Abed al-Maseeh so that they could place them in his shrine.

When Nasteer returned home he discovered that his wife now had a boy. He baptised his son at the shrine he had built. His wife told him about a vision she had seen of a man telling her that she would bear a son and that she should name her son after him. When she asked him what his name was, he told her that she would find out when her husband returned from visiting his birthplace. She told her vision to her friends, and ever since then the name of Abed al-Maseeh has spread throughout the region.

Abed al-Maseeh's father was getting old and was possessed by an evil spirit that tormented him. One day, he stood in the middle of his room and shouted loudly: "my son, Asheer, don't take revenge on me, although I deserve it". One of his sons took him to the temple and tied him to the blood-stained stone. He remained there for several days until he was cured of the evil spirit. This incident made him believe in the power of Jesus, and he was baptised in the same stream along with all his sons and his household.

There were an endless number of amazing miracles taking place at the shrine of Abed al-Maseeh. One such famous incident was of an Arab merchant who lost a herd of camels. After searching endlessly without success, he gave up hope of finding them, and in his desperation he implored Abed al-Maseeh to find his camels. He pledged that he would donate the herd to the shrine of Abed al-Maseeh. When he returned to his village, he was overjoyed to see the lost herd of camels around his house. However, greed took over him and he did not keep his pledge and decided to donate only ten camels to the shrine.

A few days later, when his servants were herding the camels, the animals went wild and ran into the wilderness with the herders on their backs. When the merchant heard of what had happened, he realised this was his punishment for breaking his promise. He gathered his friends around him and told them that he had broken a promise that he had made when he was at the shrine of Abed al-Maseeh. He begged them to go back to the shrine with gifts and beg for forgiveness for his terrible mistake. When his envoys reached the location of the shrine they pleaded for their friend. As they were praying to Abdel al-Maseeh, they saw in the distance a large number of camels approaching them. Initially, they thought it was an army heading towards them. But when they looked closely, they realised they were the lost herd of camels being led to Abed al-Maseeh's shrine. They donated all the camels to the shrine and left behind a few servants to attend to them, and then headed back to their city. To their surprise, the herd of camels started to follow them. This was a sign that Abed al-Maseeh had forgiven their owner. Many more miracles occurred in the name of Abed al-Maseeh. His feast day is celebrated by the Church on the 8 October each year.

16

Mar Patheon

Mar Patheon was born in the hamlet of Daween, near the city of Dinahoor in the province of Bet Lashbar (southern Iraqi-Iranian border), during the second half of the fourth century. His parents were practicing Zoroastrians and his grandfather, Mahryar, was a renowned Zoroastrian scholar. From his infancy, Patheon was raised in accordance with the Zoroastrian tradition and was sent to the local school to be educated. His teacher, Yacoub, secretly a Christian, had a great impact on Patheon and tried to steer him away from Zoroastrianism. Patheon decided to leave school and live with his teacher. Patheon's outraged father forced him back to school to resume his studies. However, Patheon's spirit was totally submerged in Christianity, and he asked his teacher to continue, in secret, to preach to him about Jesus, and to baptise him.

After completing his elementary education Patheon left for the city of Kirkuk (280 miles north of Iraq) in order to further his studies, but instead he found his way to the monastery of Beth Sahdaee (house of martyrs), where he was baptised by Abbot Youhanna, head of the monastery. For thirty-two years Patheon lived a monastic life based on prayer and meditation. He was finally ready to go to his hometown and preach Christianity to his own people.

When he arrived back in his village, Patheon discovered that his parents had died and only his younger brother was alive.

He converted his brother to Christianity and slowly started to influence his life. Together they headed for the nearby mountains and selected a mountain cave with its own water supply, and turned it into their new home. The two brothers yearned to convert Zoroastrians into Christians, so they left the calm solitude of their cave and started preaching in their area. Patheon performed miracles and cured many sick people. He had a considerable reputation for sanctity. People visited him and asked for his blessing and prayers. Large communities were converted to Christianity.

This was a time of persecution of Christians by the Persian rulers, known as the forty years of persecution. However, the intrepid Patheon continued to preach incessantly. During the furnace heat of the summer days, he would spend most of his time in his cool mountain cave. In winter, Patheon would head to the south of Iraq and preach around the city of Basra. He established many churches, and managed to convert many prominent and influential people to Christianity. However, they all worshipped in secret, fearing the wrath of the authorities.

As Pantheon's message was growing extensively and robustly, an inexorable wave of Christianity swept through Persian society, and the head of the Zoroastrian court, Atharfarizjird, became perturbed at its spread and the gradual demise of the Zoroastrian religion, and so he issued orders to arrest Patheon.

Patheon was brought before Atharfarizjirid, who asked him quietly, "Are you Patheon the sorcerer, head of the Christians?" Patheon replied, "I am not the head of the Christians, I am a servant of God and a servant of Christians, and I am neither a deceiver nor a sorcerer. I know the truth and I lead people to the road that takes them to eternal life." Incandescent with rage, the judge arrested Patheon. He was shackled and hurled into jail. During the night, a miracle occurred. His shackles broke open and all the jail doors were flung ajar. Patheon started walking and praying aloud; all the prisoners woke up and saw their doors open and their manacles undone. They were startled and shouted collectively: "Strong and glorified is your God, Patheon; blessed are the ones that rely on him."

The prison warden was terrified when he saw the prison doors open and when he thought that all the prisoners had escaped. The panic-stricken warden was slathered with sweat, and fear enfolded him. He began pelting himself with a torrent of curses. He knew that Atharfarizjirid would have no mercy on him, and he decided to commit suicide by falling on his sword. Patheon managed to stop him from doing so, and told him: "Do not kill yourself, Shaheen; all the prisoners are in jail and no one has escaped."

The warden rushed to see Atharfarizjirid and to tell him about the jail incident. The judge ordered Patheon to be brought before him. He screamed at Patheon: "Oh, you wicked sorcerer, even in jail you practice your magic, and you deserve to die a thousand times." Patheon replied: "I am not a sorcerer, and you know which one of us is a sorcerer. Devils befriend those that worship them. How would they help me? I am the one who fights them, and I spent all my time whipping their wickedness. All my acts are in the name of Christ; you do not see this because you are lost." Atharfarizjirid was outraged, and he ordered Patheon to be chained and thrown into the Jazan Sinee River. As Patheon was being pushed into the river, all of a sudden its waters dried up. Everyone present was amazed at how the river dried up. They murmured: "Great is your

God, and no God can match His strength and might. He is the God that sends his angels and saves his servant." Witnessing this miracle, many people converted to Christianity. Atharfarizirid claimed that this was further black magic committed by Patheon. He ordered that a large fire be set and Patheon thrown in it. Atharfarizirid's eyes became bloodshot, and he said to Patheon: "You ridicule me, O head of the sorcerers; for how long will you deceive these people by your sorcery? I will throw you into this fire, and let the God that you rely on come and save you." Patheon replied: "O, you ignorant and brainless, how could you, after witnessing such miracles, still not belief in the truth? As God sent his angels to save me from the river, he will also send his angels to save me from your fire."

As he was being lowered into the fire, Patheon started reciting the psalms. He stood unmoved by the fury of the fire that flickered about him; people watched in astonishment. Athorfarizjarid's face was etched with incredulity and anxiety. He whispered to the local leader, Nehourmzd, that if this person were to stay alive then their Zoroastrian religion would disappear from their kingdom. Nehourmzd replied: "what we are witnessing is too great; it cannot be attributed to the devils." He became very sympathetic to Patheon. Athorfarizjared replied: "It appears to me that you are a follower of this sorcerer. You will see how violently I will kill him; he will not withstand his brutal torture." Nehourmzd dared not reply, because deep down he realised that Patheon was a man of God.

Athorfarizjarid was incensed by the stubbornness of Patheon. He ordered that Patheon be taken out of the fire and put back in prison. Patheon remained in jail for two months and six days whilst Athorfarizjarid contemplated how to kill him. Athorfarizjared decided to kill Patheon in the most hideous way, known as 'the nine deaths'. His body would be cut in pieces over the course of six days. He ordered Patheon to be taken to the mountain were he worshipped his God. On his way to this mountain, Patheon was asked to renounce Christianity, but the recalcitrant monk vehemently refused. Once they reached the place where he would be tortured they asked him for the last time to renounce his Christianity. Patheon comported himself like a holy man and replied: "do not waste your time. Hurry up with my torture and obey your master's orders."

They showed him the torture instruments to scare him, but Patheon kneeled on the ground and kissed the torture instruments, saying, "I thank you, God of Heaven and Earth, for you allow me to see the instruments that will beautify my organs." His executioner immediately cut off his nose and his two ears. As they bled, Patheon held them in his hands and said, "I thank you, Lord of Heaven and Earth, for hearing me. Listen to my prayers and answer my requests; forgive my sins; let my severed organs be a sacrifice to please you and to forgive your sinful people." On the second day, they cut both his hands and his feet, and they hanged them above him. Amidst the welter of his anguish, Patheon remained silent, his thick eyebrows knotted, his lips shivering, training his narrow, foxy eyes on the distance as though he were watching something on the horizon.

On the third day, they cut off his arms, and again dangled them above him. Patheon whispered happily: "I glorify you Lord, and thank you for allowing me to carry your burden." On the fourth day, they cut his shins, and on the fifth day, they hacked his thighs. He continued to praise God whilst his torturer cut out his bodily organs and hanged them above him in his cave.

On the sixth day, the order was given to behead him. As his executioner raised his sword to cut his head,

Patheon pleaded to be given a minute for his prayer. As the last gleam of light was fading in his eyes, he said:

> O God, creator of Heaven and Earth, who hears the voices of the sinners and who accepts the requests of the penitents, hear the prayers of your servant in his last moment of life. I beseech you to listen to the prayers of the faithful who pray in my name. Grant them all they ask for, protect them from all evil, and heal their diseases in the name of your only son, Jesus Christ.

Suddenly, all present uttered the word 'Amen'. As he finished his prayer, the sword fell and he was beheaded. His bodily organs were displayed outside his cave for ten days. It was a scene of abject grief. On the 11th day, his followers gathered all his body parts and buried them on the edge of the mountain where he worshipped. The earth made his final bed.

The day of his death is recorded as the 24 October, 449 AD. Both the Chaldean and the Jacobite churches celebrate his feast day on this date. Several churches in Iraq are named after Mar Patheon.

17

Eisho Asbaran

Eisho was from the village of Koor in the mountains of Hedyab, northern Iraq. His Zoroastrian name was Mahanosh. Eisho's Christian wife managed to convert him to Christianity, and he was baptised in a monastery east of Arbeel. He became known by his Christian name, Eisho Asbaran.

Eisho was imprisoned for forty days in Hazza, but he was freed after the intervention of Yazedean, one of his friends, who was a money changer. Eisho returned to his home and built a monastery near his village. Many monks joined him, and together they lived a life dedicated to prayer, fasting and helping the poor. A large number of people converted to Christianity because of him. This caused jealousy among the Zoroastrian priests, who reported him to the governor of the region.

In 606 AD he was captured and sent to a prison in Arbeel, where he was imprisoned for 15 years. He continued with his prayers, and endured torture and insults with enormous patience. The king finally ordered his execution. He was crucified in the village of Beth Dodarie in 621. A large monastery was built in Arbeel in his name. 12 other men, noblemen from the house of Koormai, were executed along with him.

18

Patriarch Shamoun VIII Yohanna Sulaqa

he Church of the East was one of the most vibrant Christian churches in the world, its indefatigable missionaries evangelising eastward from their base in Persia and reaching as far as Korea and China.

When the Roman Empire embraced Christianity during the fourth century, this had an adverse effect on the Church of the East, meaning that its territory became divided between the competing powers at the time, the Roman and the Sassanid Empires. Under pressure from the Sassanid emperor, the Church of the East sought to distance itself from the Western (Roman Empire) Catholic Church. In 424 AD, the bishops of the Sassanid Empire held a synod under the leadership of Patriarch Dadisho (421–456 AD) and decided that henceforth they would not refer disciplinary or theological problems to any external power, and especially not to any bishop or Church council in the Roman Empire.

Throughout the thirteenth century, numerous unification initiatives were launched between Rome and the Church of the East; these moves were spearheaded by Patriarch Sabrisho V, known as Ibin Al-l Masehee (1226–1257). Western missionaries who were operating in Mesopotamia reported to Pope Innocent IV about the desires of the Patriarch to unite with Rome. However, following the Mongol invasion of the region, all efforts towards unity came to a halt.

During the reign of the Mongol Patriarch Yaballaha III (1282–1317), communication between the Church of the East and Rome resumed through an intermediary monk by the name of Souma, a close friend of the Patriarch. In 1287, Souma was dispatched to Rome as a representative of the Mongol King Argon and the Patriarch. He was warmly received in Rome, and Pope Nicholas IV dispatched a letter with him, asking Patriarch Yaballaha to join his Church in communion with Rome. In return, the Patriarch sent a letter to Pope Benedict XI through a Dominican friar named Jacob, which acknowledged the Patriarch's intention to be affiliated with Rome. However, due to war and political turmoil in the region, talks were once again halted.

Patriarch Shamoun IV Bassidi installed a hereditary system of succession to the patriarchy of the Church of the East. He ruled that his office would only pass down to members of his own family; in practical terms, to a nephew or a brother, since the Patriarch was celibate. Many individuals were consequently elected as bishops and patriarchs without any legitimacy.

When Patriarch Shamoun VII Ishoyahb succeeded his brother, either at the end of 1538 or early 1539, he made a major controversial appointment: designating his twelve-year-old nephew Hnanisho as his successor. Several years later, probably because Hnanisho had died in the interim, he transferred the succession to his fifteen-year-old brother Eliya, the future Patriarch Eliya VII. These two appointments caused a major uproar within the Church. His opponents accused him of further improprieties, such as selling ecclesiastical positions, allowing the practice of taking on concubines, selling church properties, and general intemperance.

The insouciant behaviour of the Patriarch continued to agitate the rest of the bishops, and his controversial decisions created a cocktail of dismay and resentment within his Church. A group of bishops started, surreptitiously, to look for ways to bypass his immoral and unlawful decisions. After studying in detail the Church's canonical laws of election, they were convinced that the Patriarch's new rules of hereditary succession had no legitimacy. They decided to boycott the office of the Patriarch and find a universal Church to accept them as members.

This group was headed by the Bishops of Erbil (Iraq), Salamis (Iran) and Azerbaijan. They were supported by many priests and monks. In Iraq, the dioceses of Baghdad, Kirkuk, Jazeira and Husin d'Kefa endorsed their action, and in Turkey, the dioceses of Nisibis, Mardin, Amid and Siirt backed them.

Once the bishops realised that they had a large following, they publicised their intentions and called for a general assembly of clergy, monks, and ordinary members from the disgruntled dioceses to be held in the city of Mosul (northern Iraq).

The vociferous meeting opened with warm prayers emanating from the people, longing for change. The delegates discussed the issue of hereditary nomination, and they decided to annul this law. It was agreed that a highly qualified person must be elected to serve as their patriarch. When they started to discuss suitable candidates, almost instantly and collectively they voted for Bishop Sulaqa, the abbot of the monastery of Rabban Hormizd, located near Alqosh (northern Iraq). He was regarded as an expert in canonical law, and a great visionary. A delegation was dispatched to inform him of the outcome of their meeting.

Sulaqa was born in Aqra (northern Iraq) in 1513 into a zealous Christian family. Since childhood, the allure of monastic life had enticed him, and he joined the fifty monks of Rabban Hormizd Monastery. Sulaqa was an assiduous monk with great administrative and organisational talents. The monks unanimously elected him as their abbot in 1540 at the age of 27 (the literal translation of Sulaqa in English is "Ascension").

When the delegation arrived at the monastery to inform Sulaqa of the assembly's decision, he was astonished and mystified. Sulaqa was aware of the gravity of such a decision and its consequences. He despised the busy city life, and preferred the austere solitude of his monastery. The realisation of what was to come hit him like an anvil; without any hesitation, he turned down the post and pleaded for someone else to be elected for the task.

After two more failed attempts to persuade Sulaqa, a negotiating party was sent to the monastery; and they managed to convince him to accompany them to Mosul. Upon his arrival, in 1552, he was greeted with elation and frenzied enthusiasm. The abbot was startled at these scenes, which overwhelmed his churning mind, and he succumbed to the will of the people. He was formally elected as their patriarch. Unfortunately, no bishop of metropolitan rank was available to consecrate him as a patriarch. The Franciscan missionaries urged his supporters to legitimise their position by seeking their candidate's consecration by Pope Julius III.

In April 1552, the newly elected Patriarch and his seventy companions left the city of Mosul and headed for Rome. Large crowds bade farewell to them. Some in the throng held up huge banners with messages of support. Women clutched their rosaries and wiped away their tears of joy.

Soon after their arrival in Jerusalem, Sulaqa, with three trusted men, headed for Rome. The delegation departed from Jaffa to Beirut, and, after celebrating the feast of Pentecost, they headed for Venice, arriving on 8 October, 1552. After spending some time visiting Venice's churches and places of interest, they reached Rome on 18 October, 1552.

In Rome, Sulaqa was warmly received and was given residence near the Vatican. He was inspired by this treatment, which made him forget all the hardships of his eight month journey. He prayed at the tomb of St Peter, asking the Lord to help him succeed in his mission. And, after eight days' rest, he went through the whole rigmarole of formalities, which included a detailed identity check, a test of his belief, and an interrogation of the purpose of his visit. On 20 February, 1553, he made a profession of faith to the Pope, and on 9 April, 1553, he was consecrated Patriarch in St. Peter's Basilica by Cardinal John Alvarez de Toledo, (or by the Pope, according to other sources). His appointment as Patriarch was ratified by the papal bull entitled *Divina disponente clementia*. On 28 April, 1553 he received the pallium (the sign of his patriarchal authority) from the Pope, took the traditional name of Shamoun VIII, and was proclaimed as the Patriarch of the Chaldeans. The term "Chaldeans" had been officially used by the Council of Florence in 1445 as the new name for the Nestorian Christians of Cyprus who entered in full communion with the Catholic Church. Acceding to Sulaqa's request, the Pope appointed Bishop Ambrose Buttigeg, a Maltese Dominican, as his assistant and as Nuncio to Mosul.

Sulaqa spent some time in Rome, visiting its churches and historic sites; he was flooded with joy, yet conflicting emotions swirled inside him. A barrage of questions pummelled his mind when contemplating the unknown future that awaited him. The new Patriarch bade farewell to the

Pope, who gave him some precious gifts: a golden patriarchal crown, a papal medal and a tray with cups. The
Pope also paid all the costs of Sulaqa's journey. Sulaqa then
travelled by land to Constantinople. Upon his arrival he
tried to meet with Sultan Suleiman I to discuss the affairs
of his community, but Suleiman was not in the city; then
the delegation headed for Amid (today's Diyar Baker,
Turkey), where Sulaqa wished to install the patriarchal see.

Sulaqa arrived in Amid on November 12, 1553. The city
was thick with pervading joy; the chanting and chiming
of church bells ascended from various ends of town. The
women broke into spontaneous ululations of joy. In a letter to the Pope, Sulaqa described the jubilant mood of the
people and their reception of him.

The new Patriarch felt that he had little time to achieve
so many things. As soon as the euphoria receded, he
started working vigorously by putting his old administrative skills into practice. Sulaqa knew that the destiny and
future of his new Church was dependent upon the leadership of competent individuals. The Church lacked qualified persons to organise its affairs, as the hereditary
system had left many dioceses without able bishops.

On November 19, 1553, Sulaqa ordained a new bishop
by the name of Hormuz, who took on the name of Elijah.
The second bishop he ordained was on January 27, 1554
and went by the name of Abides Bin Younan (who later
became Sulaqa's successor). Additionally, he ordained
three more bishops. In total, the Patriarch had eight bishops, including the original three who had started the
movement for unity.

The new Patriarch and his bishops took the advice of
the Apostolic Nuncio Ambrose Buttigeg, and his friends
Antonio Sahara and Father Mathew. They started an ex-
tensive theological and ecumenical renewal programme

that eliminated some of the teaching that had been forced upon the parishioners.

In December 1553, Sulaqa headed for Aleppo to meet Sultan Suleiman I. Sulaqa's community was in desperate need of the Sultan's protection. The meeting was organised by the consul of Venice in Syria, who accompanied the Patriarch. They obtained an amnesty order, issued by the Sultan to all his governors, not to harm any of this community and to treat them with respect. Patriarch Sulaqa travelled incessantly throughout the region, visiting all the episcopates under his jurisdiction. The gracious Patriarch gave the people peace from their anxiety, and he asked them to remain compliant to the authority of the Pope. His efforts bore fruit, as the new Church started to grow day by day.

Flummoxed by the turn of events within his Church, Patriarch Bar Mama responded swiftly by consecrating two more underage members of the patriarchal family as bishops: of Nisibis and Jazeera respectively. He continued with his policies, which had triggered widespread upheaval and instability within the Church. Being a man of action, and not prone to despair, Bar Mama tried furiously to obstruct the progress of the incipient Church.

Since the early part of the 16th century, patriarchs of the Church of the East had preferred Alqosh as their patriarchal seat, after which they had transferred this seat to Mar Hormuz Monastery. The area was under the jurisdiction of Hussein Beck al-Kurd, the Pasha of Amadiya. Bar Mama had an excellent relationship with the Pasha, and was aware of his greed for money. He offered him 10,000 dinars to silence the new patriarch.

The malevolent and cunning pasha plotted to get rid of Sulaqa. He invited him to visit the provinces under his jurisdiction, claiming that many of his followers were eager to see him. After giving the matter some thought, Sulaqa decided to meet with the Pasha. Almost immediately after his arrival, he was arrested and hurled into prison. He was regularly beaten and tortured by the Pasha's henchmen. Sulaqa was ordered to renounce his new communion and to obey Patriarch Bar Mama, but he refused to comply. He was later thrown in a deep well and was left there for forty days. Hunger and thirst accentuated his fatigue. The frustrated Pasha realised that he was facing an intractable challenge. He ordered his men to take Sulaqa to some nearby mountains and kill him. The Pasha would spread false rumours that he had escaped.

In the darkness and drizzle one dreary night they pulled him out of the well and shackled him to a horse. The henchmen kicked their horses into a gallop and disappeared into the night. After an hour's ride, they reached Lake Brim, near the monastery of Mar Sawa. They quickly dismounted and carried the lifeless body and threw it in the lake. This occurred on 12 January, 1555.

19

Mar Georges

One of the most famous events that God bestowed upon the Christians of Mosul was the martyrdom of Mar Georges, known as the slain (maktool) saint. Mar Georges was the son of a religious widow who had donated her house to the Dominican mission in Mosul and had re-married a nobleman from one of the rich families of the region. Mar Georges had a very religious upbringing and was known for his great wealth and chivalry.

One summer evening, after he had returned from one of his customary trading trips to the town of Dookat, he was visited by a man from the well-known family of Aga Khalid asking to borrow his horses for a journey, but Georges turned him away on the grounds that the horses were tired from his own travels. When night fell, Aga Khalid sent a man to climb over the fence and open the gate for a group of criminals to let them into Mar Georges's house to exact revenge on him.

The intruder was spotted by Father Joseph, who was sleeping on the roof of the Dominican monastery, which was next door to Mar Georges's house. Father Joseph yelled loudly: "catch him, catch him and I will hand him over to the government in the morning". But the intruder managed to get away, back to the Aga Khalid's family, and falsely accused Mar Georges of blasphemy. He told his employers that he had been captured by Mar Georges, and that when he pleaded with Georges to free him for the love of the Prophet, Georges cursed the Prophet Mohamed.

This incited the family to seek revenge, and so, led by the influential religious preacher (mullah) Yousif al-Galelie, they hurried to the government building shouting: "justice must be done." The preacher and some of his friends testified against Georges and advised that his sin would only be forgiven if he were to be killed, or if he converted to Islam. Mar Georges was captured and sentenced to death. While he was awaiting his execution, many people, Muslim and Christian, tried to intervene to save his life and seek pardon from the government, but failed because of the blasphemy charge.

In the year 1805—the exact date is unknown—Mar Georges was beheaded in the presence of a large crowd of people for refusing to renounce his religion. His body and head were gathered by one of the faithful people in Mosul and buried in the Christian cemetery. It is said that a bright light was seen emitting from his tomb and miracles took place in his name. Many sick people were healed by visiting his tomb. The Christians did not dare call him a martyr at the time, and to this day he is still known as Mar Georges the slain.

20

The Alqosh massacre

lqosh is located 28 miles north of Mosul. It lies at the foot of Beth 'Aidhre or Ba'aidhre Mountain. Alqosh is an old Assyrian settlement, most probably older than 800 BC, mentioned in the Old Testament in connection with the Prophet Nahum, who preached in Assyria between 726–697 BC and is buried there. The most distinguished religious structure in Alqosh is the Rabban Hurmiz Monastery; it is the most famous and most visited monastery in Iraq.

Rabban Hurmiz came to Alqosh Mountain after spending several years in Dair Resha (the head monastery) with his colleague Rabban Yozadaq, who also left Nuhadra Mountain. The monastery was built in 640 AD during the patriarchate of Isho-yab II (628–644 AD) with the assistance of two Ninevite princes who witnessed miraculous healing by Rabban Hurmiz. It became a famous location of learning and religion, especially during the tenth to twelfth centuries. The Rabban Hurmiz monastery, which was used as the seat for several patriarchs of the Church of the East, attracted the attention of several Muslim governors of the surrounding areas.

Between 1258 and 1401, the Mongols (after adopting Islam) and later Tamerlane (Taymorlang) attacked Alqosh and its monastery. The monks were forced to flee. Monastic life returned to the monastery a few years afterwards, but on a smaller scale.

In 1743 Alqosh was pillaged by the Persian army of Nader Shah. According to a letter dated 1746 by the priest Habash Bin Jom'aa, the writer describes the destructive acts of Nader Shah. The letter states that Nader Shah's men first attacked Karamlesh, stole its people's valuables, and kidnapped many of its children and women. Next, they attacked Bartella and committed the same acts on its Christian inhabitants. They did the same to the people of Tel Kepe (Telkaif) and Alqosh; however, many of those two neighbouring villages took refuge in the monastery of Rabban Hurmiz. Nader Shah and his troops surrounded the monastery and then attacked it as a pack of hungry wolves attacking helpless sheep. They committed some of the most horrendous crimes a human being can commit.

When Muhammad Basha (nicknamed Markoor, the one-eyed) succeeded his father in 1813 he started to strengthen his army by rigorous training regimes and buying the best available equipment. He set up many weapons and ammunition factories. To strengthen his position, in 1814 he signed a treaty with the Shah of Iran, Fateh Ali.

In 1822 he embarked on an expansion programme of his territories by invading the adjacent areas, and within 14 years he had become the most dominant and feared warlord in the region. He even annexed territories from the Ottoman Empire, but the greedy warlord was still hungry for more. He embarked on an offensive in the Mosul area.

On 15 March, 1832, Markoor's marauding army appeared around Alqosh's mountain and plains. Seeing such a large army approaching their town, the inhabitants panicked; some prominent people made efforts to calm them, but their words were hopeless. The inhabitants started to flee. Markoor was encouraged by the state of panic in the town as many defenders abandoned their positions. He gave orders to assault the town and the fleeing inhabitants. His cavalry charged with loud screams, like the bellowing of wild beasts; the horizon filled with dust; the ground shuddered; and women and children were screaming as the cavalry charged through the town, killing indiscriminately, excelling in their killing and torture and the rape of women. They entered the churches and ripped apart all the holy books—one of the damaged books is still kept in Alqosh today. The priests and deacons were slaughtered on the altars. Those who escaped to the mountains were chased by Markoor's horsemen and were butchered: amongst them was the head of the Rabban Hurmize monastery Gibrail Danbu, along with two monks and a priest. The men raised their hands in surrender but the soldiers fell upon them with daggers and swords.

The total number of people killed was 376; there were children and women, and those murdered included the town's mayor, Shmina, who refused to flee with his seven children and tried to defend the town. They killed him along with his six sons, but spared the youngest one.

On the day of this tragedy, the bishop of Amadya, Yousif Audo, was in the village; when he was captured he was severely beaten up and tortured. However, during the night he managed to escape with some companions towards the nearby mountains and hid in one of its caves. The search party discovered their whereabouts and surrounded the cave. The bishop pleaded with the soldiers, saying that they were Christians and that they payed tribute (the Jizya) to the governor of the region and that they should be spared. The soldiers took him and his companions to the tent of Markoor. The bishop showed the governor the pardon issued by the Ottoman Sultan Ali Basha that guaranteed the bishop and his Christian followers their personal safety and security of property. When Markoor saw the Sultan's order he released his prisoners and ordered his soldiers to return all their stolen possessions. He also gave the bishop a stamped paper guaranteeing his safety and his flock... but only after it was too late.

Markoor continued in his arrogance and disrespect towards the higher Ottoman authorities until the governors of Diyar Baker, Baghdad and Mosul saw him as a threat. In August 1836 they launched a major military campaign that ended up with the surrender of Markoor. He was put in chains and taken to Istanbul, where he was hanged.

21

The massacres of Bader Khan and Noorallah Beg

In 1834, Mehemet Pasha was the governor of the province of Mosul. In his quest for power he was able to convince the Porte to annex the provinces of Bahdinan and Bohtan. Bahdinan province, which includes the towns of Zakho and Amedia, was at that time nominally subject to Baghdad, and bordered upon the Tyari country in the north. Its submission took place in 1832. Bohtan was at that time subject to Diyarbakir (south-west Turkey), which comprises the whole of the district west of Bahdinan (northern Iraq) as far as Jazeera (northwestern Iraq) and west of Tyari (south east Turkey). Its submission took place in 1841.

Mehemet Pasha sent a party of his soldiers with a letter to the governor of Zakho (northen Iraq); when the meeting concluded, the governor of Zakho, his nephew and some members of household were murdered. Bader Khan Beg then refused to meet with Mehemet Pasha after the treachery practiced upon the governor of Zakho, and proceeded to build castles in different parts of the mountains and fortified himself against any sudden attack from Mehemet Pasha. The Christian Assyrians of Bohtan were the principal labourers employed on these military works, and not only were they made to serve without pay, but several of them were maimed for life by the heavy weights which they were forced to carry.

Mehemet Pasha conspired with Saeed Beg, a nephew of Bader Khan Beg, to kill his uncle, but the attempted plan failed. In 1841 Mehemet Pasha ordered a party of Barwar Kurds headed by Abdul Samad, the chief of the district of Barwar (northern Iraq) to seize flocks belonging to the Christian Assyrians, and killed several of their men and ordered several of the Bahdinan Kurdish tribes to assist Barwar's forces against the Assyrians.

Bader Khan Beg was the governor of the province of Bohtan. Bader Khan was famous for his barbarity and cruelty toward Christian Assyrians; he ruled them with an iron fist. Bader Khan resided in a mountain fortress called Deir Guli. In December 1842, Bader Khan and his commander, Ziner Beg, accompanied by lsmail Pasha, the ex-governor of Amedia, marched to the frontiers of Barwar in an attempt to throw off their subjection to the Ottoman government. They also sent a message to the Patriarch of the Assyrian Church, Mar Abraham Shamoun, requesting that he join them. But Mar Shamoun refused to join the Kurdish rebels, and expressed a sincere desire to act in accordance with the wishes of the Sultan and Mehemet Pasha of Mosul.

Noorallah Beg was the governor of the Hakkari districts (south-eastern Turkey). In 1841, the Ottoman government divided up the authority, which until then was almost entirely exercised by Noorallah Beg, between two individuals, giving to the latter the district of Bashkala, a part of eastern Hakkari, and to his nephew Sulayman Beg, jurisdiction over Julamark. The latter appointed Bader Khan as his assistant.

In May 1843, a combined Kurdish force composed of Bader Khan Beg, Noorallah Beg, lsmail Pasha and Tatar

Khan Agha declared Jihad (holy war) against Assyrians and their Christian faith, invaded the Tyari district and massacred 10,000 Assyrian inhabitants in cold blood. Many Assyrian women and children were driven into slavery and converted to Islam. Mehemet Pasha made no response to their appeal for protection for which they pleaded through the Assyrian Patriarch.

Two of the six Patriarch's brothers, as well as Father Sadook de Mar Shamoun, his two sons and his brother Yokhanan, were killed. Besides Tyari, the Kurds also attacked the provinces of Diz and Jelo. The tyrannical Kurds of Kurdistan had risen up against the Christian Assyrians and had almost put an end to their settlement in the the provinces of Tyari, Diz and Jelo. They had put the Assyrian priests and deacons to the sword, and had slain men, women and children indiscriminately. They ravished the women of Tyari and virgins in Diz. The aged mother of Mar Shamoun was seized by Kurds in Diz; they cut her body into two parts and threw it into the Zab River. All the chiefs of Tyari were killed in the massacre, as well as thirty priests and sixty deacons.

In Chomba, after the great massacre of the Assyrian Christians, Malik Ismail, the heroic chief of Tyari, was wounded and brought to Bader Khan as a prisoner. By Bader Khan's directions, the Kurds held the Assyrian chief over the river, severing his head from his body with a dagger, and cast him into the stream. Mar Shamoun, one of his brothers, two of his attendants, his father Auraha and his family made their escape to Mosul and arrived there on 27 July, 1843. Other Assyrians were less fortunate; many of those who succeeded in making their escape passed through the valley of Barwar and were captured by Abdul Samard and put to death. Abdul Samad, the chief of the district of Barwar and agent of Bader Khan, resided in the castle of Kumri, a small mud fort which could be seen from most parts of the valley of Barwar. This ruthless and fanatical chief was oppressing the Christian Assyrian population in his district by imposing high taxes on them. Ziner Beg, the commander of Bader Khan, along with 400 Kurds, invaded Ashetha and made it his headquarters, and from this strong position practiced the most barbarous cruelties upon the villages of Tyari.

The Christian Assyrians bore his tyranny patiently for some time, but in October 1843 they attacked the garrison, slew twenty Kurds, and besieged the remainder of the stronghold for six days. The Assyrians supplied the Kurds with water after the Kurds promised that they would immediately surrender and evacuate the fortress. Suddenly, however, 200 cavalry troops arrived from Bader Khan, taking the Assyrians by surprise and routing them completely; no quarter was given, and men, women and children fell in one terrible massacre.

The slaughter on this occasion surpassed the former; the village was fired, and three sacks of ears were cut off from the dead Assyrians and sent as trophies to Bader Khan. During the assault on Tyari and following the massacres of the Tyari Assyrians, Mehemet Pasha of Mosul had a large force stationed at Amedia, waiting to take possession of the country of Tyari should the Assyrians succeeded in driving out the Kurds. Asheetha was independent from the Tyari districts. In 1846 the Rayis (chief) of the village of Asheetha was Rayis Yako, and the priests of the village were Father Giwargis and Father Hormiz. Rayis Yako was seized by Bader Khan and kept as hostage during the attack on Tyari. The village of Asheetha was in a state of high alarm at the threatened invasion from Bader Khan.

Bader Khan was to march through Asheetha, and orders were sent to the Assyrian inhabitants to collect provisions for his men. His assault on Asheetha was not to be undertaken before the end of Ramadan. The descent upon Asheetha in 1843 was sudden and unexpected. The greater number of the Assyrian inhabitants fell victim to the fury of the Kurds, who endeavoured to destroy every trace of the village; the manuscripts of the churches were hid in the mountains, or buried in some secure place, but after the massacre the concealed manuscripts were not recovered, because the priests who concealed them were killed. In one area close to the villages of Minyanish and Merghe more than three-hundred Christian Assyrians were murdered in cold blood.

Lizan stood on the River Zab, which was crossed by a wicker bridge. In 1846, Lizan had a priest by the name of Kana, and he was one of the very few learned priests left among the Assyrians. The 1843 massacre at Lizan by Bader Khan Beg was horrible. Evidence of the slaughter in Lizan was clear, displayed on a platform high in the mountains covered with human remains. There were skulls of people of all ages, from unborn children to toothless old men. They were remains of those Assyrians who had been thrown from above, or who had sought to escape the sword by jumping from the rocks. When a few Assyrians escaped from Asheetha and spread the news of the massacre throughout the Lizan valley, the Assyrians of the villages round and about collected as much of their property as they could carry and took refuge on the platform, hoping thus to escape the notice of the Kurds, or to be able to defend, against any numbers, a place almost inaccessible. Women and young children, as well as men, concealed themselves in a spot which even mountain goats could scarcely reach.

Bader Khan discovered their retreat but was unable to assail it; he surrounded the place with his men, and waited until the Assyrians would be compelled to yield. The weather was hot and sultry; the Assyrians had brought but few supplies of water and provisions. After three days, the first began to fail them, and they offered to capitulate. The terms proposed by Bader Khan, and ratified by an oath on the Koran, were to surrender their arms and property. The Kurds were then admitted onto the platform. After they had taken the weapons from their Assyrian prisoners, the Kurds commenced an indiscriminate slaughter until, weary of using their weapons, they hurled the few survivors from the rocks into the Zab River below.

Out of nearly one thousand Assyrians who had congregated there, only one escaped. The heroes of the Bridge of Lizan were ten Tyari girls; these girls were led across the bridge by the Kurds, and on their return from the great massacre, preferring death to captivity and conversion to Islam, they threw themselves simultaneously into the Zab and were drowned in its waters. In 1846, the district of Tkhoma was the object of Bader Khan's fanatical vengeance, since this district escaped the 1843 massacres of the Assyrians. In the district of Tkhoma, two villages occupied opposite sides of the valley; on the right, Ghissa, and on the left, Birijai. The principal priest of Birijai was Father Hormiz. The Assyrians were in great agitation at the report of Bader Khan's march upon Tkhorna. The Assyrians at Birijai were preparing to defend themselves against Bader Khan; men carried pistols and daggers in their girdles, and long guns in their hands. The women buried their ornaments and domestic utensils in secure places; the men prepared their arms, or made gunpowder; and priests collected their books and holy vessels, to be hid in the mountains.

Among the manuscripts were many ancient rituals, forms of prayer, and versions of the scriptures; some were on vellum of a very early period. Birijai had about one-hundred houses, and Ghissa forty. The Assyrians of these two villages were comparatively rich, possessing numerous flocks, and cultivating a large extent of land. There were priests, schools and churches in both villages. The principal village of the district of Tkhoma was Tkhoma Gawaye. Malek Petros was one of the Maleks of Tkhoma.

The Tkhoma Assyrians held an assembly to discuss the expected attack by Bader Khan. After much debate it was decided to send at once a deputation to Tayar Pasha of Mosul, to beseech his protection and assistance. Two Assyrian priests, two Assyrians from families of the Maleks and two Assyrians of the principal inhabitants were chosen. A letter was written by Father Bodakh, one of the most learned and respected priests of the mountains. It was a touching appeal, setting forth that they were faithful subjects of the Sultan, had been guilty of no offence, and were ready to pay any money, or submit to any terms that the Pasha might think were fit to exact.

The letter was approved by all present, sealed with the seals of the chiefs, and delivered to the six deputies, who started out at once on foot for Mosul. At the same time, no precaution was to be omitted to place the valley in a state of defence, and to prepare for the approach of the Kurds. Gunduktha was the last village in Tkhoma. Its principal priest was Father Bodakh. Father Bodakh was an amiable, learned man, and one of the most skilful penmen; his manuscripts were much sought after for the churches. There was cause to fear that in his fanatical fury Bader Khan might attack not only the district of Tkhoma but also the district of Baz. The district of Baz contained five large villages. The Assyrians of Baz concealed their church books and property in anticipation of a disaster. The request for protection made by the Assyrians of Tkhoma to Tayar Pasha of Mosul and to the Sultan was ignored, and no effort was made by the Pasha of Mosul or the Turkish government to restrain the violence of the barbarous Kurds.

In October 1846, the united forces of Bader Khan Beg and Noorallah Beg invaded the district of Tkhoma. The Assyrians of Tkhoma, headed by their Maleks, made a heroic resistance, but were soon overpowered by numbers. An indiscriminate massacre took place. The Kurds slaughtered thousands of Assyrian men, women and children. Three-hundred women and children escaped the massacres and fled to Baz, but were surprised by Ziner Beg and brutally put to the sword in one indiscriminate slaughter; only two girls who were left for dead in the field escaped and related the sad tale of this horrible tragedy. All the villages of Tkhoma with their gardens were destroyed, and the churches were burned to the ground.

An expedition was led by Osman Pasha against Bader Khan Beg. Later, Bader agreed on terms offered by Osman Pasha to surrender his arms and move in exile to Constantinople—a punishment totally disproportionate to his numerous crimes. Although the Turkish ministers more than suspected that Osman Pasha had reasons of his own for granting these terms, they honourably fulfilled the conditions upon which Bader Khan, although a rebel, had surrendered. After Bader Khan had retired from Tkhoma, a few of the surviving Assyrian inhabitants returned to their ruined villages, but Noorallah Beg, suspecting that they knew of concealed property, fell suddenly upon them; many died under the tortures to which they were exposed, and the rest fled into Persia. This flourishing district was thus destroyed. Nooraliah Beg was later exiled to Cyprus.

22

Mar Addai Scher

Sliwa was born in Shaqlawa, northern Iraq, in February 1867 into a pious family; his father was the local priest of the village. He grew up in a religious atmosphere, and at a young age he started to help his father in teaching religious education to children. His mother died when he was at a very young age and it had a profound effect on him. In 1880, at the request of the Dominican father Jacques Rehtore, he enrolled in St John's seminary in Mosul. He studied diligently and became fluent in French, Latin, Turkish and Arabic, concentrating on philosophy and theology. After nine years at the seminary he was ordained a priest by the Chaldean Catholic patriarch Mar Elia Abu Younan on 15 August, 1889 at the Maskinta Cathedral.

He then returned to his hometown of Shaqlawa, and concentrated on teaching the young until he was recalled by Gabrail Adamo, Archbishop of Kirkuk (northern Iraq), who appointed him as his assistant. In Kirkuk he spent his time learning Hebrew, Greek, Persian and Kurdish, and he also wrote books in German and English. When Archbishop Adamo passed away in 1889, Addai was appointed as a temporary caretaker for the Eparchy. He spent most of his days teaching and serving his congregation, and at night he would spend much of his time reading and learning new languages. As a result, he became fluent in He-

brew, Persian, Kurdish, Greek, German and English. He
set up new schools throughout the Eparchy of Kirkuk.
When Bishop Yousif Khayaat was appointed as the new
Archbishop of Kirkuk, he kept Addai on as his assistant.
In 1900, Emmanuel Toma, the Bishop of Saarat, a town
in south-eastern Turkey which was until 1915 home to a
large Christian population, was elected as the new
Chaldean patriarch, after which the eparchy remained
empty for two years. On October 13, 1902, Addai was el-
evated to Bishop of Saarat.

The eparchy of Saarat was very widespread and contained many remote villages. Most of these villages were
desolate, as they had been subjected to constant attack by
Kurdish brigands because there was no authority in the
area. He worked very hard to relieve the suffering in these
villages. In 1908 he journeyed to Istanbul, where he met
the Ottoman Sultan Abdul Hamid II. From there he went
to Rome and met Pope Pius X; during his stay in Paris he
managed to make contacts with French orientalists and
print some of his works. He also managed to raise funds,
which he distributed to the poor and used to renovate his
parish. Throughout his years in Saarat, the archbishop was
mostly known for his book collection and for the cathedral's library, with its valuable collection of old
manuscripts and books. He authored works on theological, philosophical and linguistic topics.

He had a very close relationship with the Al-
Baderkhans, the local chieftains of the area, especially
with their leader, Kamel Beg. In 1915, the Ottoman army
was defeated in the Caucasus during the Great War. Ottoman Turkey started a holy war against the 'infidels' and
committed genocide that took the lives of 1.5 million
Christians—Assyrians, Armenians, Chaldeans and
Greeks. Terrible massacres took place in the area and

Christians were brutally murdered. This genocide is
sometimes also referred to as Sayfo or Seyfo, an Aramaic
word for sword.

In late 1915, Jawdad Bey, military governor of Van Vi-
layet, along with 8,000 soldiers whom he called 'The
Butchers' Battalion', ordered the massacre of almost 20,000
Assyrian civilians in at least thirty villages around Saraat.
Hilmi Beg, the governor of Saarat, informed Archbishop Addai of the impending danger to him and his
Christian flock. Addai paid the governor 400 pounds of
gold in order to save his congregation. This enabled some
of Christians of the city to flee. Addai, disguised in
Bedouin clothes, fled to the nearby mountains and hid in
one of the caves. He remained hidden for several days, but
eventually the Turkish soldiers who were looking for him
reached his hiding-place. The archbishop was brought
back to the village. He was severely beaten, sentenced to
death and finally executed. This happened in 17 July, 1915.

Eyewitness testimonies about his martyrdom

Rev Joseph Naayem, in his book *Shall this Nation Die?*
cites a witness to the last hours of Addai Scher's life:

> One day, when we were at Saraat, I was present at
> a horrible scene, the chief figure in which was His
> Grace Mar Addai, the Chaldean Catholic arch-
> bishop of that town. He was in a pitiable state, pale
> and thin. The soldiers began by jeering at him,
> pulling his beard and striking him with their rifle
> butts, firing their revolvers into the air in front of
> him. They then took the archbishop outside the
> town, and, having slain a servant of his protector,
> Osman Agha by killing him with a fatal blow to the
> head, the butchers cut off the head of the arch-
> bishop in order to show it to the governor.

The testimony of Father Paulos Pero:

His Grace was held prisoner in a government house, and he was guarded by the policeman Noor Allah bin Mawlood. He was badly treated and abused; his money and all his possessions were stolen. Osman Agha, one of the local chieftains, tried to rescue him by sending fifteen of his heavily armed fighters. They threatened Noor Allah that if the archbishop were not released they would burn his house and all his land and crops. Noor submitted to them and released Addai, and the fighters took him under darkness to Osman Agha's house. He [Agha] later took him to a nearby mountain cave. Eventually, a detachment of Turkish cavalry discovered his hideout. A fierce battle ensued between the guards and the Turkish soldiers until they ran out of bullets; they then ran away from the scene, leaving the archbishop to his fate.

The testimony of Abdu Hanna Bezir:

At the Chaldean Archbishopric of Aleppo, Syria, there is a hand-written document by Bishop Shmowel Shworez entitled "a new light on the martyrdom of Bishop Addai Scher"; it dates back to 23 February, 1963. Bishop Showrez wrote down the testimony of a gentlemen by the name of Abdu Bezir who personally met Osman Agha, a close friend of Bishop Addai. Abdu recalls: "In 1916, I accompanied a German army unit to buy equipment for boats in the village of Tanzi. There I met with Osman Agha, who told me his version of the martyrdom of Addai."

Osman Agha recalled:

> I had a very close relationship with Bishop Addai that went back to 1913. When I was sentenced to be hanged by the Turkish government, I fled to Saarat and explained to the bishop about my

predicament. He was very sympathetic to me, and he took me to the Dominican monastery were I was kept in hiding. He asked the Dominican fathers to intercede through the French consulate in Istanbul on my behalf. Due to his intervention, the Turkish government revoked my sentence and I was a free man.

When the massacres of 1915 commenced, I realised the bishop's predicament so I took my three brothers and headed for Saarat; by nightfall the bishop was safe in our village. He asked me about his people, and I told him that they were safe and hiding in the nearby mountains. I told him that I wanted to take him to Mosul so that he would be safe, but the bishop said: 'as long as my children are here I must be with them during their ordeal. I will not leave them and save myself'. I pleaded with him several times, but he refused and he went into hiding with his people. After three days, the Turkish authorities asked me to hand over the bishop to them, but I told them he escaped with his people and I didn't know where they were. I suffered so badly for my stance, as they confiscated all my possessions and land. My arch-enemy, Rasool Muhammad Agha, sent his men to search for them in the mountains. They finally caught the bishop with his people. He was arrested, and he was handed over to the Turkish authorities in the village of Tal Mishar.

The bishop asked the Turkish officer to give him some time to pray before he was shot. Rassol dragged the bishop to a nearby cave and shot him and his body was burned. He [Rassol] also killed all the Christians of Mishar, who numbered about 200 families, and stole all their possessions and confiscated their lands.

Personal letters of Mar Addai Scher

In a letter dated September 1910 addressed to his brother,
Father Petrous Scher, Addai wrote:

> My dear brother, Father Petrous Scher.
>
> Peace of the Lord and a brotherly kiss.
>
> I have not written to you for some time as I was
> not in Saarat. I was visiting the area of my Bish-
> opric, as it has some thirty-three villages. Some are
> a day's walk from Saarat, and some take up to four
> days' walking. I climbed the high mountains; the
> villagers were very excited to see me as they never
> have been visited by a bishop. They are pretty, but
> my hometown, Shaqlawwa, is prettier. My visit
> lasted thirty-eight days.

In a second letter dated July 1911 he wrote:

> My dearest Father Putrous Hanna Scher, with a
> brotherly kiss
>
> I have not written to you for a while as I was very
> busy. I am constantly attending local government
> offices to sort out my Chaldean congregation's
> problems. I am also looking after the needs of the
> Armenians and Jacobites.

23

Mar Yacoub Auraham Manni

Mar Yacoub was born in Telkaif, northern Iraq, on 3 January, 1848. At an early age he attended the church's daily services, until he heard the call to the monastic life. He joined the Chaldean Order in November 1866, at the Rabban Hurmizid monastery.

On 27 September, 1868, he professed his final vows. A year later, he was assigned to Mosul to catechise the youngsters; in the meantime, he undertook his theological training at the Patriarchal Seminary of St Peter's.

Following his ordination to the priesthood in October 1872, he returned to serve at the Monastery of Our Lady Guardian of the Fields. At the request of Mar Elia Mallos, Father Yacoub Auraham was consecrated a bishop on 25 July, 1875 by Patriarch Mar Yousif VI, Audo, and he was sent to India.

He was recalled by Rome in spring 1878, and came back to the monastery. Four years later, he was entrusted to care for the Jazira diocese, where he carried out his role with great zeal, prudence and charity. During World War One, he was detained together with other members of his clergy; a few days later they were all massacred, and his body was hauled with ropes to the Tigris River and dumped there in late August 1915.

24

Archbishop Toma Audo

rchbishop Toma was born on 11 October, 1855 in Alqosh, northern Iraq. His father was a priest and his brother was also a bishop (Israel Audo). His uncle, Yousif Audo, who was the Patriarch of the Chaldean Catholic Church, took him to Rome in 1869 to further his studies. After completing his education, he was ordained as a priest in 1880. He was appointed as assistant to Patriarch Elia Abu Younan, who succeeded Patriarch Yousif Audo.

In 1882 he was assigned to Allepo, Syria, but after three years he was recalled and appointed as a teacher in the ecclesiastical college of Mosul. During this time, he published his Chaldean dictionary, which was unrivalled by any that had been compiled before. This was printed by the Dominican printing house. Audo was ordained Archbishop by Patriarch Elia in Mosul, March 1892, and was transferred to look after the archbishopric of Urmia. Audo was an intellectual who was fluent in Arabic, Italian, French, Persian and Turkish. He was a linguistic scholar, specialising in Aramaic, and wrote or translated many books for publication.

At the beginning of the First World War, tens of thousands of Assyrians and Armenians from Anatolia found refuge in Urmia. The city changed hands several times between the Russians and the Kurds over the following two years. The influx of Christian refugees, and protection by the Russians, angered many Muslims, who attacked the Christian quarter in February 1918. The better-armed Assyrians nonetheless managed to capture the whole city following a brief battle. The region descended into chaos again after the assassination of the Assyrian Patriarch Shamoun XXI Benyamin at the hands of Simko Shikak one month later.

On 31 July, 1918, the Turkish army and Simko managed to finally take and plunder the city. Thousands of Christians—Assyrians, Chaldeans and Armenians—were massacred. Archbishop Audo was shot in the face, but remained alive until 29 August. In the cathedral of Urmia there are the remains of 4,000 martyrs who were killed in 1918.

There follows the eyewitness account of the last days of Archbishop Tomma Audo by the Rt Reverend Petros Aziz, Chaldean Bishop of Salmas.

> We three Bishops were assembled in the room of the Apostolic Delegate on the ground floor of the house. Breakfast had just been served. Suddenly, a commotion was heard at the door. The Delegate left the room to find out what was happening. At once we heard two shots, and two servants came to inform us that the Delegate had been killed. But it was they themselves who had assassinated him on the orders of their master, as was confirmed by some women who, having been in the courtyard of the mission, had been in a position to see it all.

> They had hardly gone, carrying off his body, when a Persian from the village of Balar entered and demanded money. Archbishop Audo advanced to remonstrate with him. The villain took aim and fired, and the Archbishop fell. The Persian shot him in the face, through the cheek.

Then came Saleh Effendi, and we implored him to save us. He promised, but he also demanded money. One of the priests with us guaranteed him money if he would accompany the priest to the house of a notable Mussulman (Muslim) where all the priest's belongings were stored, whereupon we all went out together from the French Mission, with Archbishop Audo, whom we thought dead, arising and accompanying us.

When we arrived at our destination, Saleh Effendi went in with the priest and left us in the hands of four Kurdish soldiers. The latter commenced to torture us in the hope of extracting money. They tore out our beards and began to lash our heads with a whip. They cut off one of Father Paul Sliwa's ears. And they promised me my life if I would return with them to the French Mission and give them anything that might still be there. Two Kurds went with me.

At the mission, a horrible sight met our eyes! In the courts, the corridors and the rooms, a crowd of infidels—men and women—armed with guns and sabres, were murdering men, women and children, after having completely stripped them. They did not shoot them, but cut them down with sabres and stilettos.

They made us walk for two hours along the roads with bare heads and feet; and, to make us keep up with the chief, who rode before us, they drove us on with blows of their whips and the stocks of their rifles. The Archbishop was exhausted.

Next day, they took us before the Commandant. There we found three others of our priests and a hundred Christians. The Commandant ordered us to be imprisoned.

Archbishop Audo was taken to the American hospital outside the town, his condition being very grave. During our detention, the massacres continued, for the Turks had granted three days and nights to the Persians to take their revenge on the Christians, and every night the whole of that week we could hear the noise of carts carrying off the bodies, which were thrown into ditches to hide them.

Archbishop Audo had remained at the hospital. Although he received medical attention, he was illtreated by the soldiers, who struck him on the head and otherwise maltreated him, so that when one day, when he came back to prison, he was a pitiable sight. Too ill to stay with us, he was taken back to hospital, where a few days later he expired. He succumbed to his injuries and died from blood poisoning.

25

The Semele Massacre

he massacre of Semele (Permit d-Semele in Assyrian) was the first of many massacres committed by the Iraqi government during the systematic targeting of Assyrians of northern Iraq in August 1933. The term is used to describe not only the massacre of Semele, but also the killing spree that continued among 63 Christian Assyrian villages in the Dohuk and Mosul districts that led to the deaths of an estimated 3,000 innocent Assyrians.

With Iraqi independence, the spiritual-temporal leader of the Assyrian Church of the East, Mar Eshai Shamoun XXIII, demanded that the Assyrians be given autonomy within Iraq, seeking support from the United Kingdom and pressing his case before the League of Nations in 1932. His followers planned to resign from the Assyrian Levies (a military force under the command of the British that served British interests) and to re-group as a militia and concentrate in the north, creating a de facto Assyrian enclave, if they were refused. In June 1933, the Patriarch was invited to Baghdad for negotiations with Hikmat Sulayman's government, and was detained there after refusing to relinquish temporal authority.

In spring 1933, Malik Yaqu, a former Levies officer, was engaged in a propaganda campaign on behalf of Mar Shamoun, trying to persuade Assyrians not to apply for Iraqi nationality or accept the settlement offered to them by the central government. His activities caused distress among the Kurds, and the Iraqi government started sending its army to the Duhok region in order to intimidate Yaqu and dissuade the Assyrians from joining his cause.

On 21 July, 1933, more than 600 Assyrians, led by Malik Yaqu, crossed the border into Syria in hope of receiving asylum from the French Mandate of Syria. Instead, they were disarmed and refused asylum, and were subsequently given light munitions and sent back to Iraq on 4 August. They then decided to surrender themselves to the Iraqi army. While crossing the Tigris at the Assyrian village of Dirabun, a clash erupted between the Assyrians and the Iraqi army. Despite having the advantage of heavy artillery, the Iraqis were driven back to their base in Dirabun. The Assyrians, convinced that the army had targeted them deliberately, attacked the army's barracks, but with little success. They were driven back upon the arrival of Iraqi aeroplanes. The Iraqi army lost 33 soldiers during the fighting, while the Assyrian irregulars took fewer casualties. Propaganda rumours circulated among Iraqi nationalist newspapers of the Assyrians mutilating the bodies of killed Iraqi soldiers, which further enraged Iraqi public opinion against the Assyrians.

Even though all military activities ceased by 6 August, stories of atrocities committed by the Assyrians at Dirabun and rumours that Christians were planning to blow up bridges and poison drinking water in major Iraqi cities spread. According to some historians, the agitation against Assyrians was also encouraged by Rashid Ali al-Gaylani's Arab nationalist government, which saw it as a distraction away from the continuous Shiite revolt in the southern part of the country.

The Iraqi army, led by Bakr Sidqi, an experienced brigadier general of Kurdish ethnicity, moved north in order to crush the Assyrians once and for all. They started executing every Assyrian male found in the mountainous Bekher region between Zakho and Duhok, starting from 8 August. Assyrian civilians were transported in military trucks from Zakho and Dohuk to uninhabited places in batches of eight or ten, where they were shot with machine guns and run over by heavy armoured cars to make sure no one survived. The town of Semele became the last refuge for Assyrians fleeing from the looted villages. The mayor of Zakho arrived in Semele with a military force on 8–9 August to disarm the city. During that time, thousands of refugees flocked around the police post in the town, where they were told by officials that they would be safe under the Iraqi flag. 10 August saw the arrival of Kurdish and Arab looters who, undeterred by the local police, took away the freshly cut wheat and barley. During the night of 10–11 August, the Arab inhabitants of Semele joined the looting. The Assyrian villagers could only watch as their Arab neighbours drove their flocks before them.

On 11 August the villagers were ordered to leave the police post and return to their homes, which they began to do with some reluctance. As they were heading back, Iraqi soldiers in armoured cars arrived, and the Iraqi flag flying over the police post was pulled down. Without warning or obvious provocation, the troops began to fire indiscriminately against the defenceless Assyrians.

Eight Assyrian priests were killed during the massacre, including one beheaded and another burned alive. Girls were raped and women violated and made to march naked before the Muslim army commanders. Holy books were used as fuel for burning girls. Children were run over by military cars. Pregnant women were bayoneted. Children were flung in the air and pierced with bayonets. Official

British sources estimate the total number of all Assyrians killed during August 1933 at around 600, while Assyrian sources put the figure at 3,000.

Historians disagree as to who holds responsibility for ordering the mass killings. The British Administrative Inspector for Mosul, Lieutenant Colonel R. R. Stafford, blamed Arab nationalists, most prominently Rashid Ali al-Gaylani and Bakr Sidqi. According to him, Iraqi Army officers despised the Assyrians, and Sidqi in particular was vocal in his hate for them. This view was also shared by British officials, who recommended that King Faysal not send him to the north during the crisis. Husry, on the other hand, blamed the Assyrians for starting the crisis, and absolved Sidqi from ordering the mass killing in Semele. He hinted that King Faysal I was the authority who might have issued orders to exterminate Assyrian males.

The massacre would eventually lead to 15,000 Assyrians leaving the Nineveh Plains for the neighbouring French Mandate of Syria and create 35 new villages on the banks of the Khabur River. August 7 officially became known as Martyrs Day or the National Day of Mourning by the Assyrians in memory of the Semele massacre.

The British Administrative Inspector for Mosul, Lieutenant Colonel R. R. Stafford, described the ensuing massacre as follows:

> Semele is on the main road to Zakho, about eight miles from Dohuk, under the administration of which qodha it came. It was the largest village in the neighbourhood and consisted of over one hundred Assyrian and ten Arab houses. The total population would have been about 700. On August 8th, the Qaimaqam of Zakho appeared with a lorry full of soldiers. No satisfactory answer has yet been given to the question why he should have come with troops into a district that was outside his ad-

ministration. He entered the village and told the Assyrians to surrender their rifles, as he feared that fighting might occur between the rebel Assyrians and the Government forces, in which case the people of Semele would be less likely to be involved if they had no rifles. Plausibly, but with lies in his heart, he assured them that they would be safe under the protection of the Iraqi flag, which flew over the police post—for Semele, being a large village, had a police post of one sergeant and four men. The Assyrians then handed in their arms, which were taken away by the troops.

Next day, more troops returned, and disarmed further Assyrians, who in the meantime had come in from the surrounding villages. The following day, the 10th, passed comparatively quietly. Nothing happened except that Arabs and Kurds could be seen looting neighbouring villages. They even came in and stripped the communal threshing floors on the outskirts of Semele, where the cut barley and wheat was stacked in piles. The unarmed Assyrians could do nothing and the police did not intervene; they explained that they had no orders and that in any case their numbers were insufficient.

It was becoming quite clear now to the Assyrians what was likely to happen. Not only had they seen this looting going on, but they suddenly found they were forbidden to draw water from the village spring, being permitted only to go to the main stream, which was dirty. They knew that the Army had already shot many Assyrians. They had seen their head priest, Sada, taken out of Semele. All day they watched the looting Arabs and Kurds. Not one of them dared to move from the neighbourhood of the police post, except one or two whose

houses were nearby, and who went to and fro on
pathetic household tasks such as the making of
bread, the last meal that many of them were destined to eat. They were now in a state of deadly
fear, and they spent that night in and around the
police post, which is built on a small hill. In the
small hours of the 11th, when the moon had risen,
the watching Assyrians began to observe their
Arab neighbours of the village starting away driving their flocks before them. This opened their
eyes beyond possibility of error. They realized the
trap they had been led into and they knew that
they were entirely helpless.

The police sergeant ordered the Assyrians from
the outlying villages to return to their homes.
When they refused, saying that it was unsafe, he
ordered them to leave the police post and go down
to the houses in the villages below. They obeyed
reluctantly. Some went to the house of Gauriel and
his brother Tinan, who kept reassuring them that
they would be safe and that the Government
would protect them.

As others were going down to the houses they suddenly saw lorries of troops and armoured cars arriving. Looking around to the police post they saw
a policeman pulling down the Iraqi flag, which
until then had been flying, as it had flown for years,
as a symbol of the law and order under which every
inhabitant of Iraq could live in safety and security.
Suddenly, and without the least warning, the
troops opened fire upon the defenceless Assyrians.
Many fell, including some women and children,
and the rest ran into the houses to take cover. Not
a soul was to be seen in the streets. The troops well
knew that there was not a rifle or revolver left in
the village. An officer then drove up in a car and

the troops came in. This officer has since been identified as Ismail Abawi Tohalla, who comes from a well-known but by no means respectable Mosul family. He shouted to the soldiers not to kill the women and children. These were ordered to come out of the houses and go up to the police post. Many did so.

A cold-blooded and methodical massacre of all the men in the village then followed; a massacre which for the black treachery in which it was conceived, and the callousness with which it was carried out, was as foul a crime as any in the blood-stained annals of the Middle East. The Assyrians had no fight left in them, partly because of the state of mind to which the events of the past week had reduced them; largely because they were disarmed. Had they been armed it seems certain that Ismail Abawi Tohalla and his bravos would have hesitated to take them on in a fair fight. Having disarmed them, they proceeded with the massacre according to plan. This took some time. Not that there was any hurry, for the troops had the whole day ahead of them. Their opponents were helpless, and there was no chance of any interference from any quarter whatsoever. Machine gunners set up their guns outside the windows of the houses in which the Assyrians had taken refuge, and, having trained them on the terror-stricken wretches in the crowded rooms, fired among them until not a man was left standing in the shambles. In some other instances the blood lust of the troops took a slightly more active form, and men were dragged out and shot or bludgeoned to death and their bodies thrown on a pile of the dead.

Gavriel, who had raised cheers for the Army at the Mosul meeting of July 11th, went out to plead for the Assyrians. He explained who he was, and said that his nephew, Ezra Effendi, had long been an officer in the Iraqi police. He showed his nationality papers, but these were torn in pieces before his face and he was shot in cold blood.

A priest named Ismail, who had taken refuge in the police post, was driven out by the police; a rope was tied round his neck and he was kicked down the steps and dragged away by the troops, who shot him, afterwards throwing his body on the steadily growing heap of corpses. Whilst this organized slaughter was going on, the police sergeant, who had from the beginning taken a leading part in the diabolical plot, ordered the Assyrian women to clean up the blood from the neighbourhood of the police post. The women complied, but only for a time. Suddenly they rebelled against this inhuman order and told the police sergeant to turn the machine guns on them, as they would rather die. The soldiers then took the men that remained down to a ditch and went on killing until every man was dead. It was then discovered that a few men had taken refuge among the women, and that some of them had hastily got into women's clothes. These were rounded up and murdered.

When there was no one left to kill, the troops took their departure. This was about two p.m., and they went off to Aloka for their midday meal and afternoon siesta. As soon as the troops had gone, the tribes, who had been interested spectators, came in and completed the looting of the houses which the soldiers had commenced. Later in the evening, the troops came back, for the police sergeant had reported by telephone that a number of Assyrian men had appeared at the police post and taken refuge there. These were hunted out and killed. The shooting went on until about sunset. In the meantime, the other houses in the village were crowded with weeping, terror-stricken women and small children. Few of them had any meal that night or for the next few days, for what grain there was in the village had been removed by the Kurds, who had also gone round the houses removing cookery utensils, bedding, and in some cases even the roof beams.

Next morning the women, already distracted beyond all reason, had a further shock when they saw the Army returning, for they did not know what this might portend. The Army, however, had merely come back to bury the dead. The bodies were collected and placed in a shallow ditch. It must be remembered that the month was August, with a daily sun maximum of 160 degrees Fahrenheit. According to the military report, 305 men, four women, and six children were buried. Many of the killed were little more than half-grown boys. Some other twenty women and children were wounded. I myself saw later one child who had been shot in both wrists as he was being held in the arms of his father who was killed.

That night and the subsequent nights some of the women were raped by the police sergeant and the soldiers. Doing everything possible to minimize what had happened, the Arabs have stated that no such incidents occurred. This is a lie. All that can be said is that throughout these terrible days there were fewer outrages on women than would have been expected. It was also everywhere stated at the time that this massacre was the work of the tribes and the irregular police. This, too, is a lie. It was the work of the Iraqi Army, disciplined troops under the direct command of their officers; the troops responsible for practically all the killing being the motor machine-gun detachments, while other troops who were passing the village throughout the day did nothing to stop what was going on.

The burial in the shallow ditch, which was carried out most inefficiently, caused the stench under the burning sun to become almost unendurable, and every fly and pestilential insect for miles around was drawn to the village. In this unspeakable atmosphere there lived, for six days, one thousand terrified women and children who had seen all their male relations killed before their eyes. All they had to eat were a few dried watermelon seeds, and they had scant water. Even at night they had little sleep, for they did not know what might be coming next. A little bread was sent from Dohuk, but nothing on an adequate scale was done until Hikmet Beg Suleiman himself on the 15th arrived in the village and was overcome by what he saw. As soon as he returned, doctors and sanitary men were sent to Semele, and the bodies were decently and properly reinterred. When I visited Semele myself with Major Thomson on August 17th few traces could be seen of what had occurred, but the sight of the women and children is one which I shall never forget—and I spent more than three years in the trenches in France! That day the women and children were removed to Dohuk, and thence, as there was no proper accommodation, to Mosul, where they were placed under canvas in a camp.

Every effort was made to hush up what had occurred, and censorship for a time was imposed on out-going letters. It was soon seen, however, that the killing could not be kept secret, for the Christians in the north had sent the news abroad, and as is the nature of things an affair of this kind was bound to get out. In fact, the details were published in the Beirut newspapers before they were known in Mosul. The Baghdad Government began to admit that there had been a slaughtering of the Assyrians, but they threw the blame on the tribes and the Irregular Police. Later this was found to be useless, and Yasin Pasha, the Iraqi delegate to Geneva, had to admit that the excesses had been committed by the regular Army. The Pasha went on to add that the excesses merited, and had received, severe condemnation. This was untrue. The troops were given triumphal receptions when they returned to Mosul, Kirkuk, and Baghdad. In Mosul the Crown Prince, who is now King of Iraq, at a great military review, was decorated with his own hands with the colours of the troops who had been engaged against the Assyrians. Bekir Sidqi, Hajji Ramadhan, and the other officers concerned were promoted. Bekir Sidqi, on his arrival in Baghdad, motored through the crowded streets amidst enthusiastic applause, sitting on the right hand of the Prime Minister.

Survivors' accounts of the massacre

Khoshaba Bercham

I was seven years old and had two brothers—one of them was still a baby. My father took us to the house of Gorial al-Bazi, as he held an Iraqi citizenship and was on good terms with the government. When we reached his house I saw many dead bodies scattered in the courtyard. Some of the wounded were being bayoneted to death. When the soldiers saw my father they shot him and he died instantly.

Mariam Sorrow

I was eight-years-old when I saw the Iraqi soldiers kill my father. He was about thirty-years-old. He told us that he would run away from us in order to distract the attention of the soldiers away from us. When the soldiers saw my father running, they started chasing him and they shot him dead. My father's uncle, Yousif and his uncle, Gewargis, were decapitated on a rock near the water well of Semele. I saw so many dead bodies.

Mariam

The soldiers entered our house and they killed my husband and my seven-year-old son David. I went berserk and started screaming at them. One of the soldiers tried to kill me, but his friend stopped him and said to him: "don't kill her, let her live in her misery by remembering her husband and son's death."

Nemo Awoo

On Tuesday, 8 August, a large number of soldiers entered Semele they collected all the weapons. The Governor of Duhok took them away and asked three Assyrians to help him. They were Father Sada and two others. When they were out of the village they were all killed. The priest was decapitated and his body was cut to pieces. On Wednesday, the Arabs stole some of our sheep and killed eight people. On the third day, the police asked three men to accompany them to search for the stolen sheep, and then they killed them after they had gone some distance from Semele. They must have been bayoneted to death, as we heard no gun shot sounds. On Friday, many soldiers appeared in the village; they entered all the houses and killed all the males.

I saw with my own eyes two officers drag a woman inside a house, and after a while she came out shaking and told her mother-in-law that they had raped her. I came to know that a nine-year-old girl managed to escape to the church. When she was discovered by the soldiers they killed her and burned her body in a pile of holy books.

Unknown woman

On 8 August, all the inhabitants of the nearby villages were told to head for Semele so that they would be protected. On 11 August, the Iraqi flag was pulled down in the police station and Iraqi army soldiers. They were accompanied by some armed tribesmen from the Shamer tribe and the Kurds of Muhamad Agha Slifani.

The soldiers rushed towards the houses and started killing all the men and children over the age of ten. Three women were killed with their children; one of them was Khamee, wife of Havil—she was pregnant and they split open her stomach. Amongst the dead were 11 priests; two of them were Chaldean Catholics, and all of them were tortured and then killed. Some six women who tried to shield their husbands were also killed together with their children. After killing all the men, the soldiers started to take all their clothes and their belongings. The army took many young women with them. To this day their fate remains unknown.

26

Father Hanna Yacoub Qasha

ather Hanna Qasha was born in 1919 in the province of Ninveh, northern Iraq, into a very religious family. After completing his high school education, he enrolled into the seminary of St John the Beloved in Mosul in 1933.

He studied diligently and immersed himself in the world of religion; his precocious brilliance was noticed by his teachers. He excelled in languages, and became fluent in Italian and French. He loved to read medical books, and became a self- taught expert in herbal medicine. On May 15, 1943, Father Hanna and five of his seminary colleagues were ordained priests by the Bishop of Amadiya, Mar Youkhanna.

Father Hanna joined the Zakho episcopate and served the Dohuk parish assiduously. He was well-liked by his parishioners. When the time for his transfer came, he was given the choice of serving in a parish near his home, but instead the young priest chose a mission in the remote mountainous areas near the Turkish border.

From his base in a Qara Wola village, Father Hanna served the villages and hamlets of Derabon, Afizrook, Ashkafidly, Bakhloja and Soriya. His motto was "Here I am, Lord, I have come to do Your will." The pious priest served in this area for a period of twenty years, travelling between these villages, despite the rugged and often harsh winter terrain. He was a man of great faith and compassion; in addition to his pastoral service, he often treated the villagers' illnesses and taught them how to read and write.

In 1958, political and social unrest grew in intensity as the Iraqi monarchy continued to distance itself from the people, and proved to be rotten to the core. A secret underground movement of free officers grew within the army, determined to topple the monarchy.

Late evening on 13 July, 1958, the 20th Brigade of the Royal Iraqi Army headed south, supposedly towards the Iraqi-Jordanian border. At 2:30 am it stopped six miles from Baghdad; then, instead of swinging south towards the border, it headed for the heart of the capital. A few hours later, Iraqis woke up to hear the radio announcing the overthrow of the monarchy and the birth of the Iraqi republic. But, far from ending the revolutionary process, the coup marked the beginning of a deeper crisis.

Factional splits between the Kurds in northern Iraq and the new central government surfaced. In 1960, discontent slowly grew amongst the bellicose Kurds, leading to a full scale revolt and open warfare. The area became turbulent. Several Christian villages and cathedrals were burned and pillaged. Despite these tragic events, Father Hanna steadfastly worked to rebuild his missions and his congregations.

The gracious priest felt the pain and unmerited ordeals of his parishioners. He visited all his villages, encouraging his flocks and giving them hope with his inspirational words and deeds. On 15 May, 1968, the day of the 25th anniversary of his ordination, he wrote to a friend:

> Today I celebrate my 25th anniversary as a priest in deep silence. I have spent 25 years of my priesthood in solitude and painful silence. Sometimes I have struggled and sacrificed with all my strength and ability. I can say emphatically and with convection that I remained steadfast and never surrendered to

despair, especially in these uncertain times. I remained steadfast, not because of my will, but because of constant prayers. Many times I faced difficult situations, but I came out more resolute and better equipped to persevere, and to endeavour to continue in my mission amongst these neglected and abandoned people in a borderless desert.

Near the village of Soriya there was an Iraqi army unit stationed around al-Assi (today's Bateel). This unit patrolled the villages of the Slefani plain intent on flushing out Kurdish rebels. The commander of this unit was a ruthless lieutenant by the name of Abd al Karim al Juhaishi. On the morning of 16 September, 1968, Father Hanna was holding mass with his congregation when a loud noise was heard. It was a mine that blew up under a military convoy four kilometres away from the village. A kind of stillness descended on the village; a heavy, cloying quiet, like the stillness before a storm.

Moments later, brutish soldiers with their commander swarmed around the village like a shoal of sharks. The village was brim-full of fear and tension. Lieutenant al Juhaishi ordered all the villagers, including Father Hanna, to be rounded up in an area known as the garlic fields. They were hardly able to stand, so great was their fright.

Father Hanna pleaded with Lieutenant al Juhaishi to show mercy, as this was a peaceful village and had never harboured insurgents. The lieutenant grew increasingly vituperative the more Father Hanna pleaded. He turned his anger on Father Hanna by beating him severely and hitting him on the head with his pistol. The blood ran in rivulets down the priest's face. As Father Hanna lay on the ground, semi-conscious, soldiers commenced firing at the screaming villagers. Many started running frantically in all directions.

Father Hanna managed to stand up, his face swathed in red blood, and pleaded again for the soldiers to stop the shooting. Lieutenant al Juhaishi was overcome with rage; an incredible torrent of abuse flowed from his mouth. He pointed his revolver at Father Hanna's head and shot him several times. The heartless lieutenant gave explicit orders to kill everyone, and participated in the execution of unarmed villagers. His victims included women, men and children.

In an effort to conceal his gruesome crime, Lieutenant al Juhaishi ordered his soldiers to place all the dead bodies inside the houses, which they covered with dry hay and set on fire. The air was impregnated by a sharp smell of burning. Clouds of smoke swirled over the village, and most of its houses were speckled with bullet holes.

When the soldiers withdrew from the smouldering village, some locals from nearby hamlets arrived and swiftly put out the fires. They discovered the lifeless body of Father Hanna, with his ruptured skull and his bloodied rosary on his chest. He was later buried at the Zakho church on 19 September, 1969.

Every night after his death, his mother wept bitterly, ardently kissing his crimson tunic. Her tears turned into a convulsive fit of sobbing; she remained in this state until she died of a broken heart. This was several months after Father Hanna was killed.

On 17 September, 2011, a Soriya Martyrs commemoration ceremony was held in Dohuk stadium. Accompanied by senior officials and dignitaries, the remains of the martyrs were then placed on military vehicles and taken to the Soriya village cemetery. The inhabitants of the village lined up, carrying flower bouquets in honour of the martyrs. A foundation stone was laid for a monument to immortalize the martyrs of Soriya village.

27

Cecilia Moshi Hanna

ister Cecilia Hanna was born in 1931 in Aradin, northern Iraq. In her early years she decided to enter the Order of Heart of Jesus to serve her people as a nun in the best traditions of Christianity. The order of Heart of Jesus was established in 1904 under the guidance of Father Ablahad Rayes, and by the year 1914 the order had already grown to a community of 10 sisters. Sister Cecilia joined the order when she was in her early teens and stayed with it till her martyrdom.

During the Kurdish rebellion of 1961, Aradin, as well as dozens of Christian villages, was caught in the crossfire between Iraqi governmental and Kurdish rebel gunfire, and was severely devastated. Sister Cecilia's family along with thousands of others were forced to move to Mosul, where she took charge of the newly established monastery. Sister Cecilia stayed there till 1999, when she moved to Baghdad to continue serving the Catholic Chaldean community and other needy people.

On August 15, 2002 three armed men entered the Sacred Heart of Jesus monastery in Baghdad, and found a solitary Assyrian nun preparing to quietly retire to her room. Seventy-one-year-old Sister Cecilia Moshi Hanna was brutally attacked by these dagger-wielding assailants and repeatedly stabbed to death. Cecilia's neck was slit and her head severed from her body. According to the medical examiner, the 70-year-old nun had been stripped naked and cruelly tortured for five hours before her throat was cut and she was beheaded.

Earlier on the evening of the attack, Sr Cecilia had been at her family home in the city until 9 pm. Her family had suggested that she stay at the family home rather than venture out into the night. However, Sr Cecilia insisted on returning to the convent so as not to leave it unattended. Ordinarily, three nuns would have been resident in the convent, but on that night none of the others were present.

It is widely believed that the three assailants had broken into the convent with the intention of murdering all three nuns normally living there. When only Sr Cecilia was found, all three attackers apparently turned their assault upon the defenceless seventy-one-year-old woman. Sr. Cecilia succumbed to the flurry of knife stabbings alone in her room. On the following day, normally a special day of retreat for nuns throughout Iraq, Sr Cecilia's fellow nuns gathered for their annual event. Noting Sr Cecilia's unusual absence, the nuns searched for her, only to discover the blood-soaked and beheaded corpse lying in her room. Her devoted friend, Sister Albertine, found her stripped naked, wrists tied to her ankles, with one leg broken. Her mouth was stuffed with rags. Her throat had been slit, and there were seven stab wounds in her torso. She had been turned to face the mosque, and there was a single dried tear on her cheek.

When Muslims built a mosque in 1998 directly across the street from the Order of the Daughters of the Sacred Heart, graffiti with slogans attacking the nuns started to appear on nearby walls, followed by rock-throwing.

Suspicion has been growing about Iraqi complicity in Sr Cecilia's murder as well, since no official outcry or condemnation has emerged from the government, even following an unusually strongly worded letter by the Chaldean Patriarch, Mar Raphael Bidaweed, wherein he states, "I strongly condemn this criminal and inhumane act on one of our Chaldean nuns in Baghdad, and demand that the officials work seriously to track down and punish those criminal thugs." The government did not conduct any investigation or issue a public statement of support for the Christian community.

One of the mothers whose son committed the vicious murder of Sister Cecilia said: "Even if my son was hanged, I would still celebrate—because he entered a Christian home and bought a place in heaven." With the killing, her son had secured an eternal reward from Allah, she believed. Her statement illustrated a depressing fact that could be seen and felt in post-war Iraq.

The killers were caught: two of them neighbours of the nuns, all extremist Muslims. But before the 2003 invasion of Iraq, Saddam Hussein released these criminals from prison. Sister Cecilia's killers came home to loud, celebratory parties. One of them lived across the street from the convent. The nuns fled their cloister with taunts in their ears. Sister Cecilia was killed on 15 August, 2002, on exactly the 98th anniversary of the establishment of her beloved Order of the Heart of Jesus. The martyred and much loved Sr Cecilia will be remembered for her tireless and unending dedication to the service of all humanity in the name of Jesus Christ.

28

Father Paulos Iskander

Father Paulos Iskander, a Syrian Othodox priest aged 59, was snatched off a Mosul street on 9 October, 2006 while searching for car parts at a local mechanic shop. The kidnappers telephoned the priest's oldest son soon afterwards, demanding $350,000 ransom from the family.

After negotiations over several more calls, the kidnappers gradually reduced their demands to $40,000, but added another stipulation: that the priest's church must publicly repudiate Pope Benedict XVI's remarks about Islam in his lecture in Germany the previous month.

The family managed to raise and pay the ransom, and the St Ephram parish of the Syrian Orthodox Church placed 30 large signboards on walls around the city, distancing itself from the pontiff's comments. But then the telephone calls stopped.

Fr Iskander's dismembered body was discovered on 11 October, at about 7 pm, in the remote Tahrir City district, 1.2 miles from the centre of Mosul. His arms and legs had been severed and arranged around his head, which rested on his chest. His remains were brought to a local hospital, which then notified his church.

Fr Iskander was survived by his wife, Azhar, sons Fadi and Yohanna, a married daughter, Fadiyeh, and a daughter, Mariam, 13.

29

Father Ragheed Aziz Ganni

ather Ragheed Aziz Ganni was born on 20 January, 1972 in Karamles, northern Iraq. In 1996 he obtained his degree in Civil Engineering and was sent to Rome, where he enrolled at the Pontifical University of St Thomas Aquinas to study Ecumenical Theology.

He was ordained a priest in Rome on 13 October, 2001 at the Pontifical Urban University, and he celebrated his first Mass in the chapel of the Irish College. Today, he is one of the nine figures represented in the apse of that chapel where relics of St Oliver Plunkett rest in the altar, wrapped in the priestly stole of Fr Ragheed. Apart from Arabic, he spoke fluent Italian, French, and English. He was a correspondent for Asia News the international agency of the Pontifical Institute for Foreign Missions.

During his study in Rome, he lived at the Pontifical Irish College and played football for the college team. The 5-a-side annual tournament played in May between the Scots, English, Beda and Irish Colleges has been named the "Ragheed Cup" in his honour. During the summer holidays, he often went to Ireland and worked at the Lough Derg Shrine in Donegal. The Irish affectionately nicknamed him "Paddy the Iraqi".

In April 2003, the Allied invasion of Iraq commenced and Saddam Hussein was ousted. Father Ragheed was enthusiastic to return to Iraq to serve Mosul's Christian

community, one of the oldest in the world, although he
expressed his opposition to the war, as he feared for the
minority Christian communities. As soon as he arrived in
Iraq, he worked vigorously for his congregation. He set up
catechist courses for the faithful of Mosul; he worked with
the young, and supported many disadvantaged families;
he even accompanied a small child with serious eye problems to undergo surgery in Rome.

As Iraq continued to lose all semblance of order, the
persecution of Christians continued in its ferocity. Father
Ragheed worked incessantly to help his people deal with
bomb attacks on churches, kidnappings, and indiscriminate killings. In his beloved city of Mosul, church bells
rang timidly and people prayed silently; he witnessed the
pain of his relatives and the loss of friends. Mosul became
a funeral city; the smell of death spread into every corner.
Father Ragheed stayed defiantly in Mosul, saying Mass day
by day in his parish.

He said:

> We will not stop celebrating Mass; we will do it un-
> derground, where we are safer. I am encouraged in
> this decision by the strength of my parishioners.
> This is war, real war, but we hope to carry our cross
> to the very end with the help of Divine Grace.

On 4 August, 2006, when 80 children of his Parish of the
Holy Spirit received their first Holy Communion, battles
broke out in the street outside, and the children cowered
from the sounds of guns and rockets.

The good shepherd helped them through. He told Asia
News:

> Although people are used to it and remained rea-
> sonably calm, they started to wonder whether they
> were going to make it back to their homes or not.

> I was aware of the immense joy of the 80 children
> receiving their first Communion, so I turned the
> subject into a joke and said to them: "Do not panic,
> these are fireworks. The city is celebrating with us."
> And at the same time I gave them instructions to
> leave the church quietly and quickly.

After an attack on his parish on Palm Sunday in 2007, he
commented:

> We empathise with Christ, who entered Jerusalem
> in full knowledge that the consequence of his love
> for mankind was the Cross. Thus, while bullets
> smashed our church windows, we offered up our
> suffering as a sign of love for God.

Then the bombings multiplied; the kidnappings of priests
in Baghdad and Mosul became more frequent. Ragheed
began to grow tired and his enthusiasm weakened, to the
point where, in his last e-mail to *Asia News* on 28 May,
2007, he admitted:

> We are on the verge of collapse. In a sectarian and
> confessional Iraq, will there be any space for Chris-
> tians? We have no support, no group who fights
> for our cause; we are abandoned in the midst of
> this disaster. What is the future of our Church? But
> I am certain about one thing, one single fact that
> is always true: that the Holy Spirit will enlighten
> people so that they may work for the good of hu-
> manity, in this world so full of evil.

On 3 June, 2007, Trinity Sunday, Father Ragheed was
killed along with three sub-deacons, including his cousin,
Basman Yousif Daud, Wahid Hanna Isho and Gassan Isam
Bidawed, in front of Mosul's Holy Spirit Chaldean Church.
The three sub-deacons had recently decided to accompany
Fr Ragheed because of threats against his life. The killers

booby-trapped the bodies so that it took hours before they could be collected.

Sub-deacon Wahid Hanna Isho's wife, Bayan Adam Bella, the only witness to the martyrdom, spoke out on the first anniversary of Father Ragheed and his sub-deacons' deaths. She recalled:

> Father Ragheed and his cousin, Sub-deacon Basman Yousef Daud, were in the lead car, and Subdeacon Wahid Hanna, myself and Sub-deacon Gassan Isam Bidawed were following in another car. At a certain point, the car was stopped by armed men. Father Ragheed could have fled, but he did not want to because he knew they were looking for him. They forced us to get out of the car, and led me away. Then, one of the killers screamed at Father Ragheed: "I told you to close the church. Why didn't you do it? Why are you still here?" And he simply responded, "How can I close the house of God?" They immediately pushed him to the ground, and Father Ragheed had only enough time to gesture to me with his head that I should run away. Then they opened fire and killed all four of them. They dragged their blood-stained bodies and placed them in the car, and boobytrapped the car with explosives, with the aim of causing further carnage should anyone come near the car to recover the bodies. In the immediate aftermath of the attack, the bodies remained abandoned on the city street, because no-one dared to approach. It was only towards ten pm (local time) that security forces finally defused the explosives, allowing for the corpses to be recovered.

At the time of his murder, Father Ganni was secretary to Paulos Faraj Rahho, the Archbishop of Mosul. Rahho was murdered only nine months after Ganni's death, in the same city of Mosul.

Thousands of people attended the funeral of the four men in Karamles, Iraq on 4 June, 2007. Despite the danger, 2,000 faithful attended the funeral masses of Father Ragheed, Sub-deacon Basman Yousif Daod, Sub-deacon Gassan Bidawed and Sub-deacon Wahid Hanna Isho. The celebrant was the Chaldean Bishop of Mosul, Archbishop Paulos Faraj Rahho. With hearts full of bitterness, the Patriarch of Babylon for the Chaldeans, His Beatitude Mar Emmanuel III Delly, and all the Chaldean bishops raised a scornful protest and denounced the martyrdom.

Father Ragheed remembered

Irish President Mary McAleese mourned the death of Father Ragheed and said:

> Father Ragheed Ganni's death challenges us to work for reconciliation between faiths and to create a world where each human life is revered. These are days of sorrow for a caring family, for a lacerated country, and for so many others. Father Ragheed returned to live and minister in the ancient city of Mosul in the Parish of the Holy Spirit in full consciousness of the risks. But Father Ragheed lived his life by a commandment to love. In our sorrow we remember, on this Feast of Corpus Christi, his sacrifice, his willing sacrifice, in service of his faith. I thank God today for the blessing that has been given us in Father Ragheed Ganni. May his faithful soul be on God's right side.

The Vatican Secretary of State Cardinal Bertone telegrammed Fr Ragheed's bishop on behalf of Pope Benedict XVI, saying that

> Ragheed's sacrifice will inspire in the hearts of all
> men and women of goodwill a renewed resolve to
> reject the ways of hatred and violence, to conquer
> evil with good, and to cooperate in hastening the
> dawn of reconciliation, justice and peace in Iraq.

A particularly poignant message was one from one of his
Muslim friends, Adnam Mokrani, Professor of Islamic
Studies at the Pontifical Gregorian University, who wrote
the day after his death:

> I ask your forgiveness for not being with you when
> those criminals opened fire against you and your
> brothers. The bullets that have gone through your
> pure and innocent body have also gone through
> my heart and soul. You not only shared the suffer-
> ing of your people but also joined your blood to
> the thousands of Iraqis killed each day. I will never
> forget the day of your ordination... with tears in
> your eyes you told me: "Today, I have died to self." I
> didn't understand it right away... but today,
> through your martyrdom I have understood that
> phrase. You have died... so that Christ would be
> raised up in you despite the sufferings, sorrows,
> despite the chaos and despite the madness.

Mgr Liam Bergin, Rector of the Pontifical Irish College in
Rome, said of Ragheed:

> I knew Ragheed for the seven years that he lived
> here as a seminarian and newly ordained priest. He
> had visited us on several occasions since returning
> to Iraq in 2003, and I had spoken with him by tele-
> phone just ten days before his death. He was pre-
> cisely as you described him: warm, good-natured,
> humorous, a fine student (previously he had gradu-
> ated as an engineer) with a grounded spirituality.
> News of his murder has shocked us greatly. His fam-

ily came to Rome for his ordination, and for his first Mass celebrated in our chapel in the presence of the Patriarch of the Chaldean Church, Cardinal Connell and Archbishop Brady. He had a great capacity for friendship, and many mourn his death. What a tragic loss it is for his parents and his siblings.

A father's tale

Even if he was not responsible for a 'miracle', I will always be grateful to Fr Ragheed Ganni.

When our son was born, he did not breathe. It is quite common for newborns to need encouragement to respire, by the nurses rubbing them manually or via the warning equipment in the birthing room, which is what happened with our second child. This time was different, and our boy didn't respond to anything when the midwife took him out of my wife's arms. Then someone in the room pressed the emergency button, and within seconds about a dozen medical professionals rushed in. But he was not responding. Then I thought I heard someone say: "He's gone into cardiac arrest."

It was then that everything turned hyper-real, as they do during moments of intense stress and panic. One cannot believe something so awful is actually happening for real. It was at that point that I got down on my knees by the bed, and for some reason the man I prayed to was Fr Ragheed Ganni, an Iraqi priest who was killed in Mosul in June 2007.

Later, the medical staff told us that our son James had taken two minutes before screaming at the top of his lungs, a sound that brought such overwhelming relief and fearless joy that I could not contain my tears and (my uncharacteristically un-English) hugs for the doctors. You can imagine how long those two minutes had felt.

James's first breaths, and the life they signified, were not a miracle by any means; because his water birth had occurred with such speed, his lungs were filled with liquid, and he survived because of perfectly explicable medical technology and the very competent and compassionate staff at the Whittington Birth Centre (it was their third such emergency that morning). But I thank Fr Ragheed anyway, and still think of his life of sacrifice, during a period of intense persecution for Christians, as a model to follow.

A week or so after the birth, and with a healthy boy whose screams by now were rather less welcome than that first magical outburst, I took a bundle of documents and hospital notes to Islington Town Hall to register the birth. We had decided on the name James, after my mother's brother, and had already chosen a couple of middle names. But I wanted another, despite my wife's protests. "You know I have to do this", I told her as I left. And so our son bears the name Ragheed on his passport, possibly becoming the first Englishman to do so. I just hope he won't hold it against me, for it will serve him as an example and guide on life's journey.

From Nineveh to Lough Derg

It was rather by accident than design that I found myself in Lough Derg the first time. The flow of life had carried me from the banks of the mighty Tigris in Iraq, to the Tiber in Rome where I study, and flowed into a remote lough and its island in Co Donegal, St Patrick's Purgatory.

I remember clearly my first day on Lough Derg, asking such questions: "what am I doing her? Am I mad? What are these people doing here? What sort of place is this exactly?" The wind, the rain, the cold weather! I remember thinking "what a place is this, yet here I am and here I must stay. I will overcome all of this and help the staff to organise the various activities around the island. Throughout the days and weeks I began to learn about the place, discovering its own particular style and history. Slowly those first impressions, a mixture of curiosity and horror, gave away to a deeper appreciation of both the rich heritage of Celtic Spirituality of the island and of the island experience, and the reason why people came and came back to the island.

I was really impressed by the devotion of the pilgrims, so much so that at the end of my work on lough Derg I decided to go on pilgrimage myself. Lough Derg is quite unique. A place where you go with heavy burdens, leaving them there touched by the hand of God.

The next year I decided to return to work on Lough Derg, I was given a job again, for five weeks this time. Now that I had experienced life on St Patrick's purgatory, I was looking forward to returning to the beautiful liturgies celebrated on the island. The liturgical action, both inside and outside the basilica evoked in me the close presence of God, his love and mercy for us all.

On the island of Lough Derg I sat watching the water being gently lifted by the wind lapping against the shore and remembered the words of the Psalmist: "By the rivers of Babylon, there we sat down and wept when we remembered Sion." I have travelled from my home by the banks of the rivers of Babylon, to a place I thought was the end of the world and to an island on a remote lake in Co Donegal. There, "at the end of the world" I have sat down and been with the pilgrims 'doing the beds', being annoyed by fasting midges I have sat—though not wept—and remembered not Sion but my home of Nineveh and above all the great thing that binds these two places together, namely the Christian faith.

Father Ragheed Ganni

30

Archbishop Paulos Faraj Rahho

Paulos Faraj Rahho was born on 20 November, 1942 in Mosul, northern Iraq. He spent nearly all his life in Mosul, a city with one of the largest and oldest Christian populations in Iraq. In 1954 he entered the St Peter's junior and major seminary in Baghdad. After his ordination on June 10, 1965 he briefly worked in Baghdad before being appointed to St Isaiah's Church in Mosul. Between 1974 and 1976, Rahho completed his religious studies, obtaining a Licentiate in Sacred Theology at the Pontifical University of St Thomas (*Angelicum*) in Rome. He worked as a priest both in Baghdad and in Mosul. He later founded the Church of the Sacred Heart in Tel Keppe, a town some 20 kilometres north-east of Mosul. He also opened an orphanage for handicapped children in 1986.

On 12 January, 2001, the Synod of Bishops of the Chaldean Catholic Church elected him archbishop of the Archeparchy of Mosul. On 16 February, 2001, he was ordained Chaldean Archbishop of Mosul, giving him responsibility for around 20,000 Catholics in ten parishes. He was ordained by the Patriarch of Babylon. His church is known in Mosul as Safina (the Ship), but parishioners called it the Holy Spirit Church.

A warm, humble and compassionate man, he was famous for his jokes—something often remarked on by his brother bishops. What no one doubted was his courage in defence of his flock. On at least two previous occasions he faced down harassment and threats. In August 2004, he was frogmarched out of his official residence and forced to watch as the building was set ablaze. On another occasion, he was accosted by gunmen in the street, but walked on, daring them to shoot him.

As well as working with other Christian leaders to show unity in the face of rising Islamic terrorism, he sought to forge good relations with local Muslims. After his residence was burned down, a local imam offered him accommodation at a mosque complex. But he also talked about the dilemmas facing Christians being pressurised to leave, convert to Islam or stay and pay the *jizyah*, a tax imposed on non-Muslims. He told Asia News:

> We, Christians of Mesopotamia, are used to religious persecution and pressures by those in power. After Constantine, persecution ended only for western Christians, whereas in the east threats continued. Even today we continue to be a church of martyrs.

By 2008, following the pacification of al-Anbar province, Mosul became the last stronghold of Sunni militias and remained the most dangerous city in Iraq. In spite of all this, Archbishop Rahho refused to leave and remained in Mosul, publicly celebrating liturgies, ministering to his flock, and openly calling for peace and reconciliation. Late on 29 February, 2008, Archbishop Rahho was kidnapped from his car in the Al-Nur district of Mosul. The gunmen sprayed the Archbishop's car with bullets, killing Faris, the driver, and Rami, the personal guard. Another companion, Samir, was wounded seriously and transferred to hospital, where he passed away. They shoved the archbishop into the trunk of a car. In the darkness, he managed to pull out his mobile phone and call the church, telling officials not to pay a ransom for his release as he believed that the money would not be paid for good works but would be used for killing and more evil acts. Other reports stated that investigators also believed the archbishop may have been shot at the time of the kidnapping.

An eyewitness account stated that the corpses had been shot in the face. "All their faces were gone when we saw them," the eyewitness said. "They were without eyes, without noses and without mouths." Each of the three men left behind a wife and three children.

The kidnappers demanded that Christians contribute to the jihad, through *jizyah*. They also demanded the release of Arab (non-Iraqi) detainees, and that they be paid three million dollars for Rahho's release. The kidnappers also demanded that Iraqi Christians form a militia to fight the US forces.

On 13 March, 2008, the archbishop's body was found buried in a shallow grave near Mosul. Officials of the Chaldean Church in Iraq said they had received a call telling them where the body was buried. Reports over the cause of death were contradictory. An official of the morgue in Mosul said the archbishop, who had health problems, including high blood pressure and diabetes, might have died of natural causes. Police at the Mosul morgue said the Archbishop "appeared to have been dead a week and his body bore no bullet wounds." Nineveh Deputy Governor Khasro Goran stated that when relatives and authorities went to the location specified by the kidnappers and found the body, it had "gunshot wounds."

The cause of death is still not known. The archbishop did suffer poor health, and was reliant on daily medication for diabetes and high blood pressure, raising the possibility—

however improbable and remote—that he may have died of more natural causes. Fr Mikhail said that when he saw the bishop two days before his kidnapping, the church leader had only been able to stand for 10 to 15 minutes at a time due to these heart problems. According to the priest, one of the main reasons for Rahho's bad health was the stress of constant threats from militant gangs demanding extortion money. "One day before his kidnapping, they attacked the bishop's house in Mosul and broke many things," Fr Mikhail said. He added that the attackers demanded a payment but the bishop refused, telling them that it was against his religion to pay money that would be used to finance violence.

Thousands attended his reburial in the village of Kremelis, an ancient Christian village near Mosul. Archbishop Paulos Faraj Rahho is believed to be the highest-ranking Chaldean Catholic clergyman to have been killed in Iraq. On 9 June, 2009, Archbishop Rahho posthumously received the 2009 Path to Peace Award awarded by the Path to Peace Foundation at the United Nations Headquarters in New York City. In his will, published by the website Ankawa.com and dated 15 August, 2003, he sends a strong message of love and brotherhood to all religious communities in his beloved Iraq, remembering with particular tenderness the disabled people cared for by the charity he founded in 1986. Here are a few excerpts from his will, translated from the Arabic by Asia News.

> None of us lives for oneself, and no one dies for oneself. For if we live, we live for the Lord, and if we die, we die for the Lord; so then, whether we live or die, we are the Lord's (Romans 14:7–8).

> Death is a dreadful reality, more dreadful than any other reality, and each one of us must deal with it. People who give their lives, themselves, their being and all they possess to God and to others express

in this way the profound faith they have in God and their trust in Him. The Eternal Father takes care of everyone and harms no one because his love is infinite. He is Love as well as Fatherhood at its fullest. This way, we understand death. Death means an end to this giving to God and others (namely in this life) in order to open up and give oneself again, without end or flaw. Life means fully placing oneself in the hands of God. In death, giving becomes infinite in eternal life.

I call upon all of you to be open to our Muslim and Yazidi brothers and to all the children of our Beloved Homeland, to work together to build solid ties of love and brotherhood among the children of our Beloved Country, Iraq.

Servant in the Gospel of Christ

Here are some of the international reactions:

Pope Benedict XVI stated that the murder was "an act of inhuman violence that offends the dignity of the human being." The Pope also denounced the 5-year-long Iraq war, saying it had provoked the complete breakup of Iraqi civilian life. "Enough with the slaughters. Enough with the violence. Enough with the hatred in Iraq!"

British Foreign Secretary David Miliband said: "His [Archbishop Rahho's] kidnapping was a cowardly act perpetrated by individuals who have rejected dialogue and peaceful politics. His killing represents an appalling act of premeditated violence. My thoughts are with the Archbishop's family."

President George W. Bush was quoted as saying "I send my condolences to the Chaldean community and the people of Iraq. The terrorists will continue to lose in Iraq because they are savage and cruel."

The Chaldean Catholic Church said: "Patriarch Emmanuel III Delly, who broke down and wept during funeral service in Karamles, urged Christians on Friday not to seek revenge for the death of the archbishop."

The Archbishop of Canterbury, Dr Rowan Williams, expressed his deep shock and sorrow at the appalling murder of Paulos Faraj Rahho, the Chaldean Archbishop of Mosul: "Our prayers are daily with the people of Iraq, especially with the vulnerable Christian community, and particularly today with the Chaldeans and Archbishop Paulos' family."

Bishop Ibrahim Ibrahim of Canada said: "He was a believer in the fraternity of all humankind." He also said: "He was very good with the Muslims" and

> He preached forgiveness for everyone. He preached that we take care of each other, without regard to faith or name or gender. He was very close to his flock, very close, especially to those who were marginalised—poor people, handicapped people.

Aftermath

One of the killers, named Ahmed Ali Ahmed, was found and arrested. Ahmed was an Al-Qaida in Iraq cell-leader based in Mosul. On 19 May, 2008, the Iraqi Central Criminal Court sentenced Ahmed to death. However, high-level representatives of the Chaldean Catholic Church opposed the death sentence. "If he were still alive, Archbishop Rahho himself would not permit someone to die for him." Chaldean Auxiliary Bishop Shlemon Warduni of Baghdad told Asia News. "Let us recall that the principles that have always inspired the Church are forgiveness and reconciliation. Violence should not call for more violence! We are on the side of justice, not the death penalty."

31

Father Adel Yousif Abboudi

Adel Yousif was born on August 14, 1961, in Baghdad. After completing his high school education, he attended the Technology University, and graduated in 1983 with a degree in Electrical Engineering. He went on to work in the Ministry of Transport. From childhood he wanted to devote his life to the church and become a priest. On October 10, 2001, his dream came true and he was ordained a priest.

He was known for his beautiful homilies. He visited all the Syriac churches in Iraq and said Mass in all of them. Father Adel helped people to deal with bomb attacks on churches, kidnappings, and indiscriminate killings. When the church of Saint Paul and Saint Peter was bombed in 2005 he went to the church of Dar al-Massara for the elderly, and later to the Mar Severus of Antioch Syriac Orthodox church. He established many prayer groups, and gave numerous talks and lectures to the young. Father Adel was married but had no children.

He was known for helping the poor, and he was elected vice-president of the Syriac Orthodox church. He was the director of a mixed high school, attended by Christians and Muslims, young men and young women. Before his assassination, Father Yousif received a number of death threats.

On Saturday, 5 April, 2008, at 11 am, as he was entering his house, he was attacked by assailants armed with guns with silencers and was shot to death in front of his shocked wife. Father Adel was struck with four bullets.

32

Tony Adwar Shaweel

A five-year-old boy, Tony Adwar Shaweel, was kidnapped by an unknown group on 3 May, 2009. He was abducted near his home in an area of Shikhan (50 kilometres northwest of Mosul in northern Iraq), and after five days the kidnapers contacted his family asking for a ransom of 50,000 US dollars.

His family pleaded desperately with the kidnappers to free their little boy, as they could not afford to pay the huge ransom. On May 11, 2009 Tony's body was discovered in the Roovya district of Aqra, near Mosul. Medical sources stated that the body had received a gunshot to the head and his body was riddled with bullets. Just another unconscionable act committed by criminals targeting Christians. Still, Iraq's embattled Christians were shocked to discover the body of the kidnapped boy.

Lt Colonel Shawkat Suleiman, chief of police in the Shikhan District, said: "this crime has been committed by criminals who like to spread terror and fear amongst the population."

Violence around the city of Mosul (regarded as the last urban stronghold of Al-Qaida) continues unabated, and Christians have been singled out by criminal gangs, Islamic extremists and other armed groups as part of a wider strategy to drive the Iraqi Christian community out of Iraq.

33

Massacre of Sayidat al-Najat Church

ayidat al-Najat (Our Lady of Salvation) is a well-known landmark in Karada, a mixed, largely middle-class district of central Baghdad. Towering above the church is a huge, modern crucifix that dominates the local skyline. It was a beacon to the faithful, until that day when brutes bristling with machine guns, grenades and suicide belts burst into the house of God.

The attack

It was 5.30 pm on 31 October, 2010 when the attackers stormed into the church, closed the doors, and started to shoot at the lights, the crucifix and the Madonna, as well as sweeping the worshippers with gunfire. They turned to a 27-year-old father, Tha'ir Abdal, who tried to plead with the attackers to stop; they shot him through the mouth and chest, yelling "we have killed an infidel." With hands outstretched, body riddled with bullets, he lifted his face to the crucifix, and his burdened soul screamed silently with anguish, "God, to thee I commend my soul."

After a four hour siege, as the Iraqi forces rushed in to confront the attackers, the gunmen opened fire on the hostages they had taken in the church, slaughtering them en masse. In the basement of the church one gunman killed 30 hostages, either by throwing two grenades at them or by setting off the explosives in the vest he was wearing.

The fierce gun battle resulted in the deaths of two priests and fifty-eight worshippers, including a four-month-old baby and a three-year-old child, with around sixty-seven others wounded. Amidst the blood, screams and terror, a three-year-old boy named Adam witnessed the horror of dozens of deaths, including those of his own parents. He wandered among the corpses and the blood, following the terrorists around and admonishing them, "enough, enough, enough." According to witnesses, this continued for two hours, until Adam was himself murdered. He remains among the youngest of Iraqi Christian martyrs. The carnage was of unprecedented cruelty and barbarity, and has left an indelible mark on the Christian community of Iraq.

The majority of the parishioners who survived the massacre have not returned to Baghdad. The horrors of that day are still etched in their memories. Some of them who were treated in France and Italy decided to remain in their newly adopted countries; others have left for Canada, turning away in disgust at the residue of violence.

The church was officially re-opened on 31 October, 2011. Some sections of the church walls that are still smeared by blood and riddled with bullets are framed by glass to bear witness to the massacre.

Eyewitness accounts

The mother of the murdered priest Father Tha'ir was proudly sitting in front of the altar with her elder son, Raed, Raed's wife and their 10-month-old daughter. Tha'ir's mother tearfully recalled:

After the second deafening explosion rocked the rear of the church I turned and saw gunmen with suicide belts strapped around their waists scrambling in through a hole they'd blown in the church doors. They were screaming "Allahu Akbar! Allahu Akbar!" [God is great]. I saw the other priest, Father Wassem, staggering close to the church's entrance, pleading with the terrorists to stop. They shot him through the mouth and chest, shouting "We've killed an infidel." When I turned around I saw my son, Father Tha'ir, fall on the steps of the altar gasping, "God, to thee I command my spirit."

I saw his blood spill across the floor. I fell to my knees and started rubbing my hand through his blood. They shot me too. They shot my hand in my son's blood. As terrified worshippers threw themselves between the pews, I saw my eldest son push his wife and baby daughter in the direction of the sacristy, where other worshipers were scrambling for shelter, before reaching out to embrace his brother. Then they shot him. Both my sons fell by the altar. I lay between them and they shot me again, in my leg. My son Raed hissed at me, "Mama, don't move, be still."

I lay between my sons, thinking that Raed was keeping quiet too, so they wouldn't know he was alive. I kept my hand in my son's blood: I caressed it as I lay there listening to the gunmen shout out "We have killed an infidel! We have killed another one! We have hostages'" as they shot more people. When their ammunition ran out, they started throwing grenades.

Hussain Nahidh, a police officer who saw the interior of the church, said:

It was a horrible scene. More than fifty people were
killed. The suicide vests were filled with ball bear-
ings to kill as many people as possible. You could
see human flesh everywhere. Flesh was stuck to
the top roof of the hall. Many people went to the
hospitals without legs and hands.

One parishioner, Rauf Naamat, said militants began by
throwing several grenades and spraying the crowd inside
the church with gunfire. After the initial violence and
chaos died down, the militants walked up to the priest celebrating the Mass, told him to lie down and shot him.

During the hours that followed, an eerie quiet descended on the building, punctuated only by quiet weeping. According to Naamat, "Most people were too afraid
to produce a sound. They feared militants would kill them
if they heard them." Naamat said he heard one of the attackers talking to what he thought was Iraqi security,
threatening to blow themselves up if Iraqi forces stormed
the building.

An Iraqi official said he talked on a cell phone with
one of the hostages during the siege. He said the
hostage described how insurgents began shooting
wildly when they went into the church, and that he
could see about forty wounded people lying
around him on the floor.

The Iraqi official who spoke by phone with one of
the hostages said he also had a four-minute phone
conversation with a militant, who demanded that
authorities release all al-Qaida-linked prisoners,
starting with the women. The official said he
judged by the militant's accent and speech that he
was not Iraqi.

Ghassan Salah, 17, had just arrived for the Sunday night
service with his mother, Nadine, and brother, Ghaswan,

when the gunmen burst through the cathedral's huge wooden doors. "All of you are infidels", they screamed at the congregation.

Then the killing began. Ghassan and seven other survivors described to the *Guardian* newspaper a series of events that have broken new ground in a country that has become partly conditioned to violence throughout eight years of war. Thar Abdallah, the priest who married al-Wafi, was first to be killed—shot dead where he stood. Gunmen then sprayed the church with bullets as another priest ushered up to sixty people into a small room in the back.

Mona Abdullah Hadad, 62, was in church with her family when the gunmen started shooting. "They said, 'We will go to paradise if we kill you, and you will go to hell'. She said, "We stood beside the wall and they started shooting at the young people. I asked them to kill me and let my grandson live, but they shot him dead and they shot me in the back." "I saw at least 30 bodies", said Madeline Hannah, 33, who was seriously wounded by gunshots. Many appeared to have been blown apart by explosions detonated by the hostage-takers, she added. "They said it was 'halal' to kill us", said Hannah, whose 10-year-old son was shot in the back. "They hated us and said we were all going to die."

Speaking through a translator, George (not his real name), said: "They did not have mercy on anyone. They gathered some of us in one corner and shot five of us. The first victim was a child and his mother simply because he was crying in fear."

The uncle of Father Tha'ir, relating what one of the survivors told him, said:

> Father Tha'ir was praying and reading a passage from the Bible when the armed men arrived. He took the Gospel in hand and held it up, saying, "In the name of the Gospel, leave them and take me.

Me for them: kill me but let the worshippers go in peace. God, to thee I command my soul."

The homily of Father Tha'ir was discovered amidst the rubble in Our Lady of Salvation church by a London parishioner who visited the church to pray for her dead mother and brother. She found the blood-stained notes and took them as a reminder of her visit. When she showed them to Father Habib Jajou of the Catholic Chaldean mission in London he recognised them as Father Tha'ir's notes for his homily.

The homily

We approach the liturgical year by contemplating upon the veneration and renewal of the Church. Guided by the mystery of Jesus, the incarnated word, the Church has become the mean and the place by which we live our Christian life. We celebrate the feast of the consecration of the Church, heralding its holiness, which springs from the Holy Trinity: from the love of the Father, the grace of the Son and the descending of the Holy Spirit.

On this Sunday, the Church invites us to contemplate upon the meaning of sacredness that is established by the Church's faith, which is based on our subconscious affirmation of Jesus's divinity and filiation. Indeed, the "Son of Man" has two meanings: firstly, a Human one, because Jesus is the Son of Joseph the carpenter; and secondly, a Divine one. Jesus utters the honorific "Son of Man" in reference to himself every time he reveals His Divinity. Therefore, it is important to elucidate the meaning of the Scriptures to enable us to apprehend their theological and ecclesiastical meaning.

Jesus is the new Word and the new Mind. Jesus Christ is a human being and God in one person. Through Him, a true encounter between Human and God occurs. Jesus directs our thoughts to a new dimension; it is neither theoretical nor theological, but a call to turn to martyrdom via the cross. We acknowledge Jesus by three intermingling ways: the Holy Bible, which comprises the Word of God; the Church, which encompasses the Body of Christ; and finally the life of the faithful, which is a true nest for faith.

I am only a little boy; I do not want to die

One of the survivors of this carnage was an 11-year-old year boy, Majid Mazeen Mahrook. In his letter to the well-known Christian publication *Al Fiker Al Masehi*, he described his ordeal and some of the events that took place in the church. Majid wrote:

> I went with my parents and my sisters, Farah and Meerna, to church for our prayers. As we were making our way into the church, Father Wassem talked to my father about a possible job for my sister Farah. The Mass was conducted by Father Tha'ir; after reading the Gospel and during his homily we heard a series of explosions. Father Tha'ir told us: do not be alarmed; let's all pray together. We heard a much louder explosion, and immediately people surged into the church. I said to my mum: "are they police?" She said, "no, they are terrorists"'
>
> When they started shooting at people, I realised that they were terrorists. They killed Father Tha'ir and Father Waseem and ordered us to get into groups. I was with my father and Farah; my mum and Meerna were in another group. My father whispered to me, "do not be scared, Majoodi, God is with us." We lay down on the church floor; as my father clutched me and my sister he was hit by a

bullet in his shoulder. My sister told me about it, as I was too scared to open my eyes. I kept them closed all the time; I could only hear the whistling hiss of the bullets, then I heard a sound of a very close bullet. Farah told me that our father had been hit again, this time in his back. Farah started weeping loudly. I heard one of the terrorists shouting: "anyone that cries or moves will be killed". Farah was quiet and I was petrified. I said to God: "I am only a little boy; I do not want to die."I kept repeating all the time: "Lord, we are in your care."

As the explosions grew louder, so did the yelling of the terrorists; they told us: "you are worshippers of the cross" and "death to all Christians". The terrorists were gratuitously tormenting and killing the worshippers. We stayed for a long time in the church until the police arrived and got us out. As they were evacuating us, I could see they had lights on their helmets; I saw my father with a bullet wound in his back, his shirt drenched in blood.

I told the police to get me out with my father, but they dragged me out on my own. I found out that my mother was also wounded in her back; she is with my sister Farah in France getting treatment. I discovered that many people were wounded and killed on that day. I loved Father Tha'ir and Father Waseem and I cry a lot for them. Father Wassem taught us the Syriac Language and Father Tha'ir used to read and explain the Bible to us. I am very saddened for both of them; they are in Paradise with Jesus. Also, I always pray for my father and mother.

When night approaches and it is time to sleep, I remember everything that took place on that day and I feel terrified. I continuously have bad dreams; in one of my nightmares I am shopping in a mall with my mum and sisters. We are buying new clothes for my sister Farah and suddenly we hear a deafening explosion and we all hide in the changing room. In my other nightmare, when my mum and I press a green button dead bodies appear and we start to cry.

My dad's condition is serious and he is still in an intensive care unit [Majid was not aware that his father died in the carnage]. I miss my mother a lot, and I want to go to France to see her.

The accusations against the Iraqi police

Iraqi bloggers and even some politicians have openly criticised the Iraqi government for its handling of the attack.

They point out that the terrorists brought explosives and weapons to the church in cars with dark-tinted windows and no license plates, vehicles that are only available to officials with high-level security clearance. This allowed them to get waved through checkpoints without being stopped.

They also point to the slow reaction of the security forces, and the botched handling of the rescue attempt itself. It still remains unclear how many of the victims were killed or wounded by the Iraqi rescue team, who opened fire wildly once they burst into the church.

A senior officer in the Iraqi police, who asked not to be identified because of the sensitivity of the subject, said that for the ten days before the attack the Interior Ministry security forces gradually moved barriers closer to the church, until they were so near that the terrorists were able to drive right up to the front.

Yohanna Josef, a local resident, said:

There was an outside door to the side chapel, where some people were hiding. They [the security forces] could have gone in through that door and rescued many people; instead, they burst in through the front doors and shot everyone on sight.

Abu Udai's account

My son called me at 5:15pm when the attackers went into the church, so I told him to hide. At 5:30 I called my son again, and he said that the attackers were shooting randomly and killing people, and I heard the shooting as a background noise during the phone call; this was the last time I was able to speak to my son.

I made it to the church at 6:00pm; an Iraqi officer helped me get close to the church. I saw smoke coming out of the church, and the police and the army were all around there by the hundreds, but they were just sitting and doing nothing: in fact they looked like they were chit-chatting as if nothing was happening.

From 6:00pm till 8:30pm there was killing inside the church while the army and police outside did nothing; they were just standing there. Every 15 minutes there would be shooting and then quiet. I told the officers that I knew about the back stairs of the church and could help them get in, but no one listened. Until the terrorists had expended all their ammunition, nothing was done.

Most of the top-ranking officers were doing nothing, just sitting around and chit-chatting, and they even told me not get aggravated (because there were only twenty people in the church). I got furious and gave the names of eight of my family members inside.

When the SWAT team arrived at 9:00 pm still nothing was done by either the police or the army, while the terrorists kept killing people; even after the SWAT arrived and went into the church the terrorists did not have any ammunition anymore, and even when they went in, it was a mess and they may have killed more innocent people.

Arrests of the perpetrators

The Iraqi police made their first arrests by accident, when the passengers of a sedan aroused their suspicions at a checkpoint. Inside the car they found CDs that contained videos of the attack. The suspects eventually led the police to a Baghdad safe house where they arrested the 27-year-old 'wali', or 'prince', of al-Qaida in Iraq, an Iraqi named Huthaifa Sattar al Battawi. Battawi led the police to nineteen additional safe houses where the group had hidden large quantities of explosives, pistols fitted with silencers, car bombs and suicide vests. Battawi said they had chosen Our Lady of Salvation Church because it was located in Baghdad's central Karrada neighbourhood, close to the offices of international media organisations. "Most of what we need to accomplish for our mission in such an operation is media attention."

During a failed attempt to escape in May 2011, Battawi and ten other senior al-Qaeda militants were killed. On 2 August, 2011, three other men were sentenced to death and a fourth to twenty years in prison in connection with the massacre.

Glossary of names

Abidisho: servant of Jesus

Arbeel: present day Irbil, northern Iraq

Abed al Maseeh: servant of Christ

Azzad: free

Barsabbae: son of the dyers

Belad :   Land

Brikhisho: blessed Jesus

Eisho: Jesus

Elia: Elijah

Henannya: the mercy of God

Malek: chief

Mar: is a title of respect, literally meaning 'my lord'. It is given to all saints and is also used before Christian name of bishops.

Mattie: Matthew

Pasha: an honorary title in the Ottoman Empire, typically granted to governors, generals, dignitaries.

Rabban: Monk

Shamoun: Simon

Yacoub: Jacob

Youhanna: John

Yousif: Joseph

Sources and References

Christianity in Mesopotamia

1. Farid Oufi, "Early Christians in Mesopotamia, the first two centuries" in *Mesopotamia*, issue 11, Year 2 (July-August 2008).

2. Massoume Price, "A Brief History of Christianity in Iran" (December 2002) on www.iranchamber.com.

3. Fr Albert Abbouna, *History of the Eastern Syriac church*, I, third edition (Beirut: Dar al-Mashriq, 1993).

4. Dr Wassan Hussein, "Ambassadors of Jesus in the Arabian peninsula" in *Nagm al-Masriq*, Vol XVIII/4, no.72 (2012).

5. Andrea Di Genua, Emanuela Marinelli, Ivan Polverari, Domenico Repice, "Judas, Thaddeus, Addai: possible connections with the vicissitudes of the Edessan and Constantinopolitan Mandylion and any research perspectives."

6. Metropolitan Dr Mar Mikhael of Edessa, www.eastern-catholicchurch.org.

Koukhi

1. Farid Oufi, "Early Christians in Mesopotamia, the first two centuries" in *Mesopotamia*, Issue 11, Year 2 (July-August 2008).

2. Father Yousif Habi, *The Church of the East* (Baghdad: al-Mashriq, 1988), p.142.

Persecution of Christians

1. "The Early Years of Sassanid Empire and Religious Turmoil in Persia" on www.iranchamber.com.

2. John Stewart, "Persecution of the Persian Church under the Sassanid" in *Nestorian Missionary Enterprise* (Edinburgh: T & T Clark, 1928), pp. 17–35.

3. Massoume Price, "A Brief History of Christianity in Iran" (December 2002) on www.iranchamber.com.

4. Samuel Hugh Moffett, *A History of Christianity in Asia.* Volume I: *Beginnings to 1500* (New York: HarperCollins, 1992).

5. James R. Russell, "Christianity in Pre-Islamic Persia: Literary Sources" in *Encyclopædia Iranica*, vol. V, fasc. 5 (Costa Mesa, 1991), pp. 327–28.

6. Mark Dickens, "Nestorian Christianity in Central Asia" as found on www.oxuscom.com.

7. Richard Cavendish, "Constantine won a great victory on October 28th, 312" in *History Today*, Volume 62, Issue (10 October 2012).

8. Ronald S. Stafford, *The Tragedy of the Assyrians* (Piscataway, NJ: Gorgias Press, 2006).

9. Ian Lantham, "Christians encounters with Islam in history and modern times: some theological reflections" in *Living Stones Yearbook 2015* (Living Stones of the Holy Land Trust, 2015).

10. Suhail Qasha, *History of Iraq's Nasara* (Baghdad: Shafiq print house, 1982).

11. "Christians under the Caliphate. The Christian community under the Abbasid caliphate (750–1258)" on www.message4muslims.org.uk

12. "Siege of Baghdad, May–9 July 1401" on www.historyofwar.org.

13. Wilhelm Baum and Dietmar W. Winkler, The Church of the East, a concise history (London: Routledge Curzon, 2003).

14. Archbishop Habib Jajou, *The History of Christianity in Southern Mesopotamia* (Basra, Iraq, 2015).

1. Sultana Mahdokht

1. Father Alber Abbouna, *Martyrs of the East* (Baghdad: Al-khlood printing house, 1985), volume 1, p. 86.

2. Brothers Jonah and Brikhisho

1. Father Alber Abbouna, *Martyrs of the East* (Baghdad: Al-khlood printing house, 1985), volume 1, p. 100.

3. Mar Mehna and the six martyred virgins.

2. Archbishop Addai Scher, *History of the most famous Eastern martyrs* (Mosul: The Dominican Fathers Monastery, 1906), Volume II, p. 366.

4. Mar Shamoun Barsabbae

1. Father Alber Abbouna, *Martyrs of the East* (Baghdad: Al-khlood printing house, 1985), volume 1, p. 105.

5. Tarbow and her sister

1. Father Alber Abbouna, *Martyrs of the East* (Baghdad: Al-khlood printing house, 1985), volume 1, p. 120.

2. Rev. Alban Butler, *The Lives of the Fathers, Martyrs, and Other Principal Saints* (New York: BartelbyCom, 2010), "April 22: SS. Azades, Tharba, and Many Others, Martyrs in Persia".

6. Shahdost

1. Father Alber Abbouna, *Martyrs of the East* (Baghdad: Al-khlood printing house, 1985), volume 1, p. 164.

7. Youhanna and Father Yacub

1. Archbishop Addai Scher, *History of Chaldo and Athur* (Beirut: The Catholic Jesuit printing press, 1912), Volume II, p. 79.

8. Mar Abraham

1. Archbishop Addai Scher, *History of the most famous Eastern martyrs* (Mosul: The Dominican Fathers Monastery, 1906), Volume II, p. 263.

9. Mar Henannya al-Arbelee

1. Archbishop Addai Scher, *History of the most famous Eastern martyrs* (Mosul: The Dominican Fathers Monastery, 1906), Volume II, p. 263.

10. Mar Berhadsheba

1. Archbishop Addai Scher, *History of the most famous Eastern martyrs* (Mosul: The Dominican Fathers Monastery, 1906), Volume II, p. 268.

11. Mar Qardakh

1. E. S. Lassu, *Mar Qardakh the martyr* (Nisibeen printing press, second edition 2012).
2. Father Alber Abbouna, *Martyrs of the East* (Baghdad: Alkhlood printing house, 1985), volume 1, p. 150.

12. Mar Behnam

1. Bishop Francis Jhoola, *Life of the martyrs Behnam and Sarah* (Baghdad: Al-diwan print house, 2005).
2. Father Yousif Habi, *The Church of the East* (Baghdad: al-Mashriq, 1988), pp. 142, 308.

13. Father Yacoub and deacon Azzad

1. Archbishop Addai Scher, *History of the most famous Eastern martyrs* (Mosul: The Dominican Fathers Monastery, 1906), Volume II, p. 327.

14. Eithallaha

1.   Archbishop Addai Scher, *History of Chaldo and Athur* (Beirut: The Catholic Jesuit printing press, 1912), Volume II, p. 82.

15. Mar Abid al- Masseh

1.   Archbishop Addai Scher, *History of the most famous Eastern martyrs* (Mosul: The Dominican Fathers Monastery, 1906), Volume II, p. 77.

16. Mar Petheon

1.   Archbishop Addai Scher, *History of the most famous Eastern martyrs* (Mosul: The Dominican Fathers Monastery, 1906), Volume II, p. 373..

17. Eisho Asbaran

1.   Archbishop Addai Scher, *History of Chaldo and Athur* (Beirut: The Catholic Jesuit printing press, 1912), Volume II, p. 239.

18. Mar Sulaqa

1.   *Nagm al-Mashriq*, issue 23,vol.V, 2000
2.   *Nagm al-Mashriq*, issue 24,vol.VI, 2001
3.   *Nagm al-Mashriq*, issue 25,vol.VII, 2001
4.   *Nagm al-Mashriq*, issue 26, vol.VIII, 2001

19. Mar Georges

1.   Archbishop Addai Scher, *History of Chaldo and Athur* (Beirut: The Catholic Jesuit printing press, 1912), Volume II, p. 230.

20. The Alqosh Massacre

1. Fred Aprim, *El-Qosh (Alqosh), Yimma d'Athor (Mother of Assyria)* in Zinda X/27 (27 August 2004).
2. Bishop Yousif Babana, *Alqosh across history* (Duhok, Iraq: Oriental Cultural Centre, second edition, 2012).

21. The massacres of Bader Khan

1. Ronald S. Stafford, *The Tragedy of the Assyrians* (Piscataway, NJ: Gorgias Press, 2006).
2. George Davis (ed.), *Genocides against The Assyrians* (Chixcao, 1999).
3. Austen Henry Layard, *Nineveh and its Remains* (New York: Praeger, 1867), Volume I.
4. George Percy Bager, *The Nestorians and their rituals* (London: Joseph Masters, 1852).

22. Addai Scher

1. Joseph Naayem, *Shall This Nation Die?* (New York: Chaldean Rescue, First Edition, 1920).
2. *Bayen al Nahrain*, issue 141–142, Vol.36, 2008, p. 125.

23. Mar Yakub Auraham Manni

1. *Liturgical Calendar of St. Thomas the Apostle*, USA.

24. Bishop Tomma Audo

1. Joseph Naayem, *Shall This Nation Die?* (New York: Chaldean Rescue, First Edition, 1920).
2. Reinhard Backes, "Iran: Christians in Urmia—new life after death and expulsion" on *ACN News* (19 June 2013).

25. Semele massacre

1. Ronald S. Stafford, *The Tragedy of the Assyrians* (Piscataway, NJ: Gorgias Press, 2006).
2. Sebastian De Courtois, *The Forgotten Genocide: Eastern Christians, the Last Arameans* (Piscataway, NJ: Gorgias Press, 2004).
3. Audisho Malko Ashitha, *Semele Catastrophe in 1933, its local and international causes and influences* (Duhok, Iraq: 2013).

26. Father Hanna Yacoub Qasha

1. *Al-Qeethara*, Volume 18, issue 100, Nov–Dec 2009
2. Majed Eshoo, "Assyrian villages and Monasteries" in *Zelga* (13 August 2008).

27. Sister Cecilia Hanna

1. Ronald Boyd-MacMillan, "The Cry of Iraq's Church" in *Charisma Magazine* (31 July 2003).
2. thebloodofthemartyrs.blogspot.it/2010/04/murder-of-sister-cecilia-moshi-hanna.html
3. www.chaldeansonline.org/chaldeanews/chaldean_nun.html

28. Father Paulos Iskander

1. Dr Hanna Aydin Dayroyo, "Fr. Boulous Iskander Beheaded in Mosul" on http://www.socmnet.org/index8.htm.

29. Father Ragheed Ganni

1. Ed West, *The Silence of Our Friends: the Extinction of Christianity in the Middle East* (Ebook: 2013).
2. Pat Buchanan, "The Martyr of Mosul" (21 June 2007) on www.creators.com/opinion/pat-buchanan/the-martyr-of-mosul.html

3. www.asianews.it/news-en/The-Chaldean-Church-mourns-Fr.-Ragheed-Ganni-and-his-martyrs-9443.html

4. Adnam Mokrani , "A Muslim Friend's Letter to Slain Father Ragheed" on "www.zenit.org/en/articles/a-muslim-friend-s-letter-to-slain-father-ragheed

5. "Father Ragheed Ganni 1972–2007" on *ACN* at www.acnuk.org/father-ragheed-ganni-1972–2007?handle=father-ragheed-ganni.html

6. Cardinal Sean Brady, *Homily at Irish College Chapel Dedication* (8 December 2010) on http://www.irishcollege.org/college-chapel/dedication-chapel/

30. Archbishop Faraj Raho

1. *Obituary* in The Times (14 March 2008).

2. "Paulos Faraj Rahho: a modern martyr" (10 February 2015) on vmntblog.com/2015/02/paulos-faraj-rahho-modern-martyr.html

3. news.bbc.co.uk/1/hi/world/middle east/7294078.stm

4. "The East- Aramean Chaldean bishop Paulus Faraj Raho killed in Mosul" (3 March 2008) on www.iraqichristians.org/English/East-Aramean_Chaldean_Bishop_Killed_13_3_2008.htm

5. *Al-Qeethara*, religious and cultural magazine, the Chaldean Catholic Mission, Vol 16, Number 91, May–June 2008.

31. Father Yousif Adel Abboudi

1. Elias Bejjani, "Iraqi Christians: Exodus, Ethnic Cleansing & Identity Annihilation" (7 April 2008) on http://www.10452lccc.com/elias.english08/aboudi.elias 7.4.08.htm.

2. Ernesto Londoño, "Assyrian Priest Fatally Shot in Baghdad, Alarming Christians" in *Zinda* magazine (6 April 2008)

3. www.asianews.it/index.php?l=en&art=11952&size=A

4. *Al-Qeethara*, religious and cultural magazine, the Chaldean Catholic Mission, Vol 16, Number 91, May–June 2008

32. Tony Adwar

1. Anne Thomas, "5-Year-Old Christian Boy Kidnapped, Killed in Iraq" in *The Christian Post* (16 May 2009).

33. Sayidat al-Najat

1. Ken Timmerman, "Were Iraqi Security Forces Involved in Baghdad Church Massacre?" On *Newsmax* (1 March 2001).

2. *Fikir al-Masihi*, issue 461–462, February 2011, p. 11

3. John Leland, "Iraqi Forces Storm a Church With Hostages in a Day of Bloodshed" in *New York Times* (31 October 2010).

Lightning Source UK Ltd.
Milton Keynes UK
UKOW08f1539110517
300981UK00002B/91/P